JANE EYRE

A Dramatization
by
ROBERT JOHANSON

Based on the Novel
by
CHARLOTTE BRONTË

Dramatic Publishing
Woodstock, Illinois • London, England • Melbourne, Australia

*** NOTICE ***

The amateur and stock acting rights to this work are controlled exclusively by THE DRAMATIC PUBLISHING COMPANY without whose permission in writing no performance of it may be given. Royalty fees are given in our current catalog and are subject to change without notice. Royalty must be paid every time a play is performed whether or not it is presented for profit and whether or not admission is charged. A play is performed any time it is acted before an audience. All inquiries concerning amateur and stock rights should be addressed to:

DRAMATIC PUBLISHING
P. O. Box 129, Woodstock, Illinois 60098

COPYRIGHT LAW GIVES THE AUTHOR OR THE AUTHOR'S AGENT THE EXCLUSIVE RIGHT TO MAKE COPIES. This law provides authors with a fair return for their creative efforts. Authors earn their living from the royalties they receive from book sales and from the performance of their work. Conscientious observance of copyright law is not only ethical, it encourages authors to continue their creative work. This work is fully protected by copyright. No alterations, deletions or substitutions may be made in the work without the prior written consent of the publisher. No part of this work may be reproduced or transmitted in any form or by any means, electronic or mechanical, including photocopy, recording, videotape, film, or any information storage and retrieval system, without permission in writing from the publisher. It may not be performed either by professionals or amateurs without payment of royalty. All rights, including but not limited to the professional, motion picture, radio, television, videotape, foreign language, tabloid, recitation, lecturing, publication, and reading are reserved.

©MCMXCVIII by
ROBERT JOHANSON

Based on the Novel by
CHARLOTTE BRONTË

Printed in the United States of America
All Rights Reserved
(JANE EYRE)

Cover design by Susan Carle

ISBN 0-87129-821-X

IMPORTANT BILLING AND CREDIT REQUIREMENTS

All producers of the Play *must* give credit to the Author(s) of the Play in all programs distributed in connection with performances of the Play and in all instances in which the title of the Play appears for purposes of advertising, publicizing or otherwise exploiting the Play and/or a production. The name of the Author(s) *must* also appear on a separate line, on which no other name appears, immediately following the title, and *must* appear in size of type not less than fifty percent the size of the title type. *On all programs this notice should appear:*

"Produced by special arrangement with
THE DRAMATIC PUBLISHING COMPANY of Woodstock, Illinois"

With grateful appreciation to the first "Jane" and
"Rochester"—Elizabeth Roby and Tom Hewitt—

    and to the Paper Mill Playhouse
    for the exquisite first production.

FROM THE AUTHOR AND FIRST DIRECTOR

Adapting and directing Charlotte Brontë's incredible novel, *Jane Eyre*, for its initial production at the Paper Mill Playhouse, was a memorable and exciting experience. The character of Jane is so fresh and compelling and, I believe, so often misrepresented in various film and television versions. She is not by nature mousy or passive, but fiercely intelligent and quite aggressive for a woman of that time. She simply is plain—very plain. Charlotte Brontë herself was plain, and as a plain woman, she was forced to accept many oppressive situations, but she patiently and thoughtfully worked to bring about change. In this way, Charlotte and Jane are one and the same. Do not make the mistake of creating a Jane that is a wallflower. Use the life of Charlotte Brontë as a guide and carefully examine her novel to understand the true character of Jane. The play is Jane's story. A memory play told from the time Jane returns to the ruined Thornfield as an adult and remembers the experiences that have brought her to this place. Therefore, the production can be as abstract as you desire. It does not require huge sets for each location, but merely the suggestion. Costuming, however, should be as accurate as possible. Production notes and suggestions follow at the end of the text. The most important thing about any production is that you keep it fluid—constantly moving—changes of scene should take just as long as it takes for Jane to speak the transition speech written for her. If the show moves, you will be able to tell the entire story this adaptation attempts. All other versions that I know, tend to leave out huge portions of the novel and I believe this is a mistake. Each episode in the story builds Jane's character and eventually makes believable the epiphany of the ending. I so admire Charlotte Brontë—her writing and her difficult and inspiring life. I've tried very hard to do justice to her most famous heroine and I hope, if you produce this play, you will attempt to do the same.

JANE EYRE

A Play in Two Acts
For 7 Men and 16 Women, with doubling
(or as many as 11 Men, 33 Women and extras)

DRAMATIS PERSONNAE

JANE EYRE (as an adult)
YOUNG JANE EYRE, age 10

AT GATESHEAD:
MRS. SARA GIBSON REED, Jane's aunt
  Her children:
    JOHN REED, age 14
    GEORGIANA REED, as a child, age 12
    GEORGIANA REED, as an adult
    ELIZA REED, as a child, age 13
    ELIZA REED, as an adult
  Her maids:
    BESSIE
    MISS ABBOT
MR. REED'S GHOST

AT LOWOOD SCHOOL:
MR. BROCKLEHURST, the headmaster
MISS MILLER
MISS SCATCHERD
MADAME PIERROT, the French teacher
HELEN BURNS, age 14
MISS MARIA TEMPLE
MRS. BROCKLEHURST, the headmaster's wife
AUGUSTA BROCKLEHURST, their daughter
SCHOOLGIRLS, ages 8-17

AT THORNFIELD:
MRS. FAIRFAX, housekeeper
JOHN, waiting man
LEAH, maid
ADELE VARENS, Rochester's ward, age 9
GRACE POOLE, a servant, age 40
MR. EDWARD ROCHESTER, age 35
BLANCHE INGRAM
LADY INGRAM, her mother
MARY INGRAM, her sister
LOUISA ESHTON, sister to Amy
AMY ESHTON, sister to Louisa
SIR GEORGE LYNN
LADY LYNN, his wife
HENRY LYNN, their son
FREDERICK LYNN, another son
RICHARD MASON, from the West Indies
A GYPSY
BERTHA MASON ROCHESTER
MR. WOODS, the clergyman
MR. BRIGGS, the solicitor

AT MARSH END:
WOMAN ON THE ROAD
WOMAN AT THE DOOR
HANNAH
ST. JOHN RIVERS, age 28
MARY RIVERS, his sister
DIANA RIVERS, his sister

AT MORTON:
ROSAMUND OLIVER
SCHOOLGIRLS

THE PLACE: Northeast England.
THE TIME: 1832-1842.

SUGGESTED DOUBLING BREAKDOWN
as performed in the original Paper Mill Playhouse production. There are endless possibilities and it can be done with less than indicated here.

WOMEN
Jane Eyre (as an adult)
Mrs. Fairfax, Miss Abbot, Miss Pierrot
Sara Reed, Mrs. Brocklehurst, Lady Lynn, Woman at Door
  (cover Hannah, Lady Ingram)
Lady Ingram, Miss Scatcherd, Hannah
  (cover Fairfax, Mrs. Reed)
Blanche Ingram, Miss Temple, Bertha Rochester
  (cover Woman at Door, Woman on Road)
Miss Miller, Frederick Lynn, (cover Temple)
Rosamund Oliver, Louisa Eshton, Lowood Schoolgirl
  (cover Miller, Georgiana, Eliza)
Bessie Lee, Lowood Schoolgirl, Woman on Road
Diana Rivers, Amy Eshton, Lowood Schoolgirl
  (cover Jane Eyre)
Mary Rivers, Mary Ingram, Adult Georgiana Reed, Lowood Schoolgirl (cover Blanche, Rosamund, Bertha)
Leah, Adult Eliza Reed, Lowood and Morton Schoolgirl
  (cover Bessie Lee, Diana & Mary Rivers)

YOUNG GIRLS
Young Jane Eyre, Morton Schoolgirl
Adele Varens, Augusta Brocklehurst, Morton Schoolgirl
Helen Burns, Morton Schoolgirl
Young Georgiana Reed, Lowood and Morton Schoolgirl
Young Eliza Reed, Lowood and Morton Schoolgirl

Lowood and Morton Schoolgirls
  (out of this group comes covers for Young Jane, Helen, Adele, Georgiana, Eliza, Leah)

MEN
Edward Rochester
St. John Rivers, Grace Poole
Richard Mason, Lowood Doctor, Mr. Reed's Ghost
 (cover Rochester, Brocklehurst)
Servant John, Lowood Cook, (cover Briggs, Woods)
Mr. Brocklehurst, Sir George Lynn, Mr. Woods
Henry Lynn, Mr. Briggs (cover St. John, Grace)

BOY
John Reed, Thornfield Servant

* John Reed could be played by a girl who then doubles in the school scenes.

* Grace Poole was played by a man in this production. This could be a separate character altogether or doubled differently with a woman and St. John Rivers could play a different male role in Act One such as Mr. Brocklehurst.

* Miss Miller played Frederick Lynn—this could be played by John Reed and Miss Miller absorbed by one of the other ladies.

* If cast size is too large some roles could be eliminated such as Frederick Lynn and Amy Eshton—it is important that the party have an even number of guests so that Jane is the "odd man out"—but it could be reduced by even two more if absolutely necessary.

JANE EYRE was first produced by the Paper Mill Playhouse in Millburn, N.J., in February, 1997, with the following cast:

Elizabeth Roby .... Adult Jane Eyre — Sarah
Blythe Auffarth .... Young Jane Eyre, Schoolgirl (Morton) — Sam
Nancy McDoniel .... Mrs. Sarah Reed, Mrs. Brocklehurst, Lady Lynn, Woman at Door — Steph
Justin M. Restivo .... John Reed — Duncan
Grace Ann Pisani .... Young Georgiana Reed, Schoolgirl (Lowood/Morton) — Kelin
Laura Benanti ...... Adult Georgiana Reed, Mary Ingram, Mary Rivers, Schoolgirl (Lowood) — Marg
Lauren A. Wanko .... Young Eliza Reed, Schoolgirl (Lowood/Morton)
Julie Georgia Thomas .... Adult Eliza Reed, Leah, Schoolgirl (Lowood) — Susie
Ruth Moore .... Bessie, Woman on Road — Katie
Mikel Sarah Lambert ...... Miss Abbot, Madame Pierrot, Mrs. Fairfax — Susie
Ronald H. Siebert .. Mr. Reed, Richard Mason, Fight Captain — Duncan
William Ryall .... Mr. Brocklehurst, Sir George Lynn, Mr. Woods — Lydia
Nancy Auffarth .... Miss Miller, Frederick Lynn
Maureen Sadusk ... Miss Scatcherd, Lady Ingram, Hannah — Marg?
Natalie Van Kleef ...... Helen Burns, Schoolgirl (Morton)
Glory Crampton .... Miss Maria Temple, Blanche Ingram, Bertha — Lydia
Amanda White ...... Augusta Brocklehurst, Adele Varens, Schoolgirl (Morton) — Steph
Rahale Berman .... Schoolgirl (Lowood/Morton)
Courtney Blaine Dunn ...... Schoolgirl (Lowood/Morton)

Anne Hathaway............ Schoolgirl (Lowood/Morton)
Julie-Anne Liechty ..... Louisa Eshton, Rosamund Oliver, Schoolgirl (Lowood)
Jacqueline Macri .... Schoolgirl (Lowood/Morton)
Jennifer Lynne Marguilis .... Schoolgirl (Lowood/Morton)
Karen Phillips.............. Amy Eshton, Diana Rivers, Schoolgirl (Lowood)
Jessica Waxman .... Schoolgirl (Lowood/Morton)
John A. Andrews................................John
J. Petitchamps.......................... Grace Poole
Tom Hewitt .... Mr. Edward Rochester
Edward Staudenmayer .... Henry Lynn, Mr. Briggs
John Littlefield .... St. John Rivers

PRODUCTION STAFF

Executive Producer................... *Angelo Del Rossi*
Artistic Director .... *Robert Johanson*
Director........................... *Robert Johanson*
Scenic Design .... *Michael Anania*
Costume Design .... *Gregg Barnes*
Lighting Design .... *Tim Hunter*
Music................................. *Albert Evans*
Sound Design .... *David Paterson*
Hair Design...................... *Howard Leonard*
Fight Direction .... *Rick Sordelet*
Stage Manager .... *Lora K. Powell*
Assistant Director .... *Patrick Parker*

ACT ONE

SCENE 1: THE RUINS OF THORNFIELD HALL

AT RISE: *MUSIC: A folk-like, melancholy tune. Fog. Mist. A WOMAN dressed in black walks through the ruins—stone ramparts, chimneys, door frames, rubble. A long veil covers the WOMAN's face and upper body. She moves from the ruins, toward the AUDIENCE—slowly lifting her veil. She is a very plain woman—JANE EYRE.*

JANE *(profoundly moved by the devastation around her).* It is hard to put into words my feelings at this moment. Everything that has brought me to the place where I now stand, every action in life, every person known to me, every desire, every tear, every silence—stands with me here—begging my understanding. The veil is lifting and I am seeing and feeling what I never thought possible. Never. The lonely child that was once me, never foresaw this future.

(YOUNG JANE emerges from behind her, carrying a book—"Bewick's History of British Birds." Simultaneously, MRS. REED enters with her children, GEORGIANA, ELIZA, and JOHN, clustered about her.)

SCENE 2: GATESHEAD HALL

MRS. REED. Jane, I regret that I really must exclude you from the privileges intended for contented happy children like my darlings. You are an orphan—for nine years a guest in our home—and should dispose yourself in a more attractive and sprightly manner. Though my late husband was your mother's brother, you can no longer trade on that relationship to be unruly and disagreeable.

JANE and YOUNG JANE. But what have I done?

MRS. REED. I don't like questioners, Jane. There is something truly forbidding about a child who takes up her elders in that manner. Until you can speak pleasantly, remain silent. Children, you will keep Jane at a distance. I will not have your naturally sweet dispositions tainted by her sullenness.

GEORGIANA, ELIZA, JOHN. Yes, mama.

(MRS. REED leaves them. YOUNG JANE sits and opens her book. JOHN, after making sure his mother has gone, looks to his sisters meaningfully. He is large and stout for his age with unwholesome skin, the golden-curled GEORGIANA is quite pretty, if a little plump, ELIZA is severely handsome.)

JANE. John Reed bullied and punished me; not two or three times a week, but every moment he was out of his mother's sight.

(MUSIC: Piano or harpsichord. MRS. REED playing in the music room. Her children are now once again alone with YOUNG JANE.)

JANE. He should have been away to school, but my aunt claimed he must remain at home due to his delicate health. I feared him with every nerve in my young body.

JOHN. What now, Madam Mope?

YOUNG JANE. What do you want?

JOHN. Say "What do you want, Master Reed?"

YOUNG JANE. What do you want, Master Reed?

JOHN. I want you to come here!

JANE *(as YOUNG JANE slowly walks toward JOHN)*. I knew he would soon strike, and while dreading the blow, I mused on his disgusting and ugly appearance. I'm sure he read the notion on my face.

JOHN *(striking YOUNG JANE hard across the face)*. That is for your impudence in answering mama awhile since and for that look you just had in your eyes! *(He snatches YOUNG JANE's book.)* How dare you steal MY book— you dependent! Everything in this house belongs to me, or will do in a few years time. I'll teach you. *(He strikes her hard with the book. She falls to the ground.)*

YOUNG JANE. Wicked and cruel boy! You are like a murderer—a slave driver—you are like the Roman emperors!

JOHN. What!—Eliza! Georgiana! Did you hear what this rat said to me? *(He pulls her up by the hair and hits her hard again. The SISTERS run off screaming for their mother. JOHN throws himself on the ground and pulls the nearly fainted YOUNG JANE onto him and struggles with her as though she is attacking him.)* Help! Get her off me! MAMA! MAMA!

(MRS. REED runs shrieking into the room, followed by the maids, BESSIE and ABBOT, and her GIRLS.)

MRS. REED. Pull her off! She's attacking my delicate John! *(BESSIE and ABBOT lift YOUNG JANE off. MRS. REED kneels by her sobbing son.)*

BESSIE.	ABBOT.
Dear! Dear! To fly at Master John that way!	Did ever anyone see such a picture of passion!

MRS. REED. Lock her up in the red room!
MAIDS. The red room?
MRS. REED. She will stay there until I come to let her out. *(The MAIDS drag YOUNG JANE away. As MRS. REED supports her sobbing son to walk:)*
JOHN. Mama, why does she always attack me? *(Screams.)* Don't let her hurt me again!
YOUNG JANE. No! No! Please! I didn't do it!
JOHN. She's a liar! Liar! *(He is gone. YOUNG JANE is placed on a bench in:)*

SCENE 3: THE RED ROOM

JANE. Unjust! Cried my reason! Unjust!
ABBOT. Hold her arms, Bessie, she's like a mad cat!
BESSIE. For shame, Miss Eyre, to strike at your young master!
YOUNG JANE. Master! Am I his servant?

ABBOT. You are less than a servant for you do nothing for your keep. If Mrs. Reed were to turn you out you would go to the poorhouse.

YOUNG JANE. She is my aunt—they are my cousins!

ABBOT. Don't think yourself equal with the Misses and Master Reed. They will have a great deal of money and you will have none. It is your place to be humble. Now will you sit still or shall we tie you up? *(Preparing to remove her garters for bonds.)*

YOUNG JANE. No, no, please. I'll be still.

BESSIE. What we tell you is for your own good, Miss Jane. Try to behave. Come, Miss Abbot, I'm scared to stay in this haunted place.

YOUNG JANE. Haunted?

BESSIE. Mr. Reed's bedroom, miss.

ABBOT. He died in that bed, nine years ago. *(They both cross themselves, then exit. Locking the door.)*

JANE *(standing directly behind her younger self)*. Even from a distance of so many years, I still feel the heat of that ceaseless inward question—WHY? Why did I suffer thus?

(BESSIE and ABBOT appear in a hallway.)

BESSIE. Poor Miss Jane is to be pitied, Abbot.

ABBOT. If she were a nice pretty child like Miss Georgiana, one might pity her forlornness; but one really cannot care for such a plain little toad as that. *(BESSIE and ABBOT exit.)*

JANE. I was hated because I was plain. But, I could not see it then, all I could see was that I was in the room where my dead uncle had laid in state—my dead uncle that if he had lived would have treated me kindly.

(MUSIC: Eerie and mysterious.)

JANE. Bessie had told me that if dead men in their graves were troubled that their last wishes had not been fulfilled, they would revisit the earth to exact a punishment. I stared at the bed willing my dead uncle to save me—to save me from this hell!

(Suddenly from up out of the bedcovers, MR. REED rises reaching toward YOUNG JANE. [This can also be accomplished by merely hearing his voice.])

MR. REED'S GHOST. Jane! Jane! JANE!
YOUNG JANE *(screams and bolts for the door)*. Help! Help! Bessie! Let me out! Take me out! Save me!

(The sound of the door unlocking. BESSIE and ABBOT enter. The GHOST has disappeared.)

BESSIE.	ABBOT.
Miss Eyre, are you ill? Are you hurt?	What a dreadful noise!

YOUNG JANE. I heard the rushing of wings—I saw it! There was a ghost!
BESSIE. Haunted!
ABBOT. Another naughty trick!

(MRS. REED appears—her CHILDREN crowded behind her.)

MRS. REED. What is all this? She was to be left here until I let her out.

BESSIE. She screamed so loud, ma'am.

MRS. REED. Let go her hand! Leave this room! I abhor artifice; even in children.

YOUNG JANE. I saw my uncle Reed.

MRS. REED. What?

YOUNG JANE. My uncle Reed, he knows how you've treated me—all of you; he knows how you shut me up, and how you wish me dead.

MRS. REED *(after a stunned silence)*. You shall remain here the entire night!

YOUNG JANE. No, Aunt! Please don't! Please! Don't lock me in! *(She runs to the door as it is slammed again, leaving the sobbing and frightened YOUNG JANE alone. Imagining all sorts of horrors, she faints dead away. The lights fade.)*

JANE. I ought to forgive my aunt. She believed me to be a troubled and wanton child. To her I was. But to her I owe much mental suffering.

SCENE 4: THE HALLWAY AT GATESHEAD

(BESSIE unlocks the door and lets YOUNG JANE out.)

BESSIE. Come, Miss Jane, Missus said I was to bring you out. Don't cry, Miss Jane.

YOUNG JANE. I cry because I am miserable.

BESSIE. Missus was rather too hard. Here, I brought you your little doll. *(YOUNG JANE grabs her doll and hugs it to her.)*

JANE. With what absurd sincerity I doted on this shabby little scarecrow of a doll. I could not sleep unless it was folded in my nightgown. Human beings must love something.

YOUNG JANE. Bessie, they all hate me. Master John struck me. He struck me, Bessie, several times. What can I do?

BESSIE. Have you no other relatives, miss?

YOUNG JANE. My aunt once mentioned there might be some poor relations somewhere.

BESSIE. You might be happier with poor relations.

YOUNG JANE. I don't know that I should like to be poor.

BESSIE. Or wouldn't you like to go to school?

YOUNG JANE. I should like to very much.

SCENE 5: GATESHEAD PARLOUR

(MRS. REED sits on a couch by the fire with JOHN lying indolently beside her eating candy. A tall, sable-clad, severe gentleman, MR. BROCKLEHURST, stands across the room. GEORGIANA eats chocolates and ELIZA writes in her account book.)

JANE. My aunt, it seems, had come to the same conclusion. I was summoned to her presence.

MRS. REED. Mr. Brocklehurst, this is the girl respecting whom I applied to you. Jane Eyre.

BROCKLEHURST. Well, Jane Eyre, are you a good child?

MRS. REED. Perhaps the less said on that subject the better.

BROCKLEHURST. No sight so sad as a naughty little girl. Come here. Do you know where the wicked go after death?

YOUNG JANE. They go to hell.

BROCKLEHURST. A pit full of fire. Should you like to fall into that pit and be burning there forever?

YOUNG JANE. No, sir.

BROCKLEHURST. What must you do to avoid going to hell?

YOUNG JANE. I must keep in good health and not die.

BROCKLEHURST. You have a wicked heart. You must pray to God to change it.

MRS. REED. Mr. Brocklehurst, I know this girl has not quite the character you would wish, but should you admit her to Lowood School, please request her teachers to guard against her worst fault—deceit. She has been known to lie.

JANE. Already my aunt obliterated any hope for a new phase of my existence.

BROCKLEHURST. She shall be watched, Mrs. Reed.

MRS. REED. She should be brought up to be useful and humble. As to vacations, she will, with your permission, spend them at Lowood. *(She has written a check and handed it to BROCKLEHURST.)*

BROCKLEHURST. Perfectly so, madam. Little girl, here is a book entitled the "Child's Guide"; *(He hands YOUNG JANE a copy of the book.)* read it carefully, especially the part accounting the sudden death of Little Martha, a naughty child addicted to lying. We will expect you quite soon. Good day to you then.

MRS. REED. Good day. I will be sending her as soon as possible. *(BROCKLEHURST departs. To YOUNG JANE:)* You may return to the nursery. *(YOUNG JANE stands staring at her, calmly.)* Why do you stand there?

YOUNG JANE. I am not deceitful; if I were I should say I loved you; but I do not love you: I dislike you the worst of anybody in the world except for your son, John Reed. And as to this book, you may give it to him, for it is he who tells lies, not I. I will never come to see you when I am grown up; and if anyone asks me how I liked you, I will say the very thought of you makes me sick and that you treated me with miserable cruelty.

MRS. REED. How dare you affirm that, Jane Eyre?

YOUNG JANE. How dare I, Aunt Reed? How dare I? Because it is the truth. You think I have no feelings and that I can do without one bit of love; but I cannot live so. People think you are a good woman, but you are bad; hard-hearted. YOU are deceitful to tell Mr. Brocklehurst I have a bad character.

MRS. REED. Children must be corrected for their faults.

YOUNG JANE. Deceit is not my fault! You deceived your own husband when you promised to take care of me as your own. Send me to school soon for I hate to live here. *(YOUNG JANE leaves the parlor. MRS. REED is quite shaken.)*

MRS. REED. Oh, I will indeed.

JANE *(as lights fade on MRS. REED)*. If I had only known the depths of my aunt's deceit at that time.

(MUSIC: SCHOOLGIRLS singing the hymn—"Walk With Me"—as BESSIE buttons YOUNG JANE's black coat.)

Act I JANE EYRE 23

SCENE SIX: LOWOOD SCHOOL

(The SCHOOLGIRLS and TEACHERS bring on benches, a desk, easels, a globe and two high stools as BESSIE and YOUNG JANE bid farewell in a pool of light.)

BESSIE. Missus said she would not be down. She told the children it was not fit to associate with you.

YOUNG JANE. They are not fit to associate with ME.

BESSIE. And so you're glad to leave, then?

YOUNG JANE. I am glad to leave Gateshead, but not you, Bessie.

BESSIE. I believe I am fonder of you than all the others.

YOUNG JANE. You never showed it.

BESSIE. I daresay now, if I were to ask you for a kiss, you wouldn't give it me.

YOUNG JANE. Bend your head down. *(BESSIE does. YOUNG JANE kisses her. BESSIE grabs her into a hug.)*

JANE. Even for me life had its gleams of sunshine.

(YOUNG JANE marches directly into Lowood School. MISS MILLER meets her and removes her coat and gives her the uniform of Lowood. A bell tolls. About twenty SCHOOLGIRLS have assembled at benches running around the periphery of the room. They stand motionless and erect as MISS SCATCHERD inspects them. MISS MILLER and MADAME PIERROT, the French teacher, stand ready. YOUNG JANE has been handed a slate and chalk and directed to stand at the end of one of the benches.)

JANE. Lowood was a charity school. My aunt paid but fifteen pounds a year to send me there, the rest was made up by subscriptions from local benevolent-minded ladies. Most of the subscription money going to Mr. Brocklehurst. That very morning the meager breakfast of burned porridge was as nauseous as rotten potatoes. Not one of the girls was able to eat it. So they went hungry. Also that morning the basins were frozen so no one was able to bathe.

SCATCHERD. Helen Burns!

(SCATCHERD addresses HELEN BURNS, pale and angelic, with naturally curly red hair. HELEN stuffs a book, "Rasselas," in her workbag.)

HELEN. Yes, Miss Scatcherd.

SCATCHERD. Hold your head up. I will not have you before me in that attitude. Show me your hands. *(She does.)* Stand forth! Undo your collar! *(HELEN approaches as SCATCHERD addresses the other STUDENTS.)* Be seated! *(SCATCHERD then proceeds to beat HELEN's back with her pointer.)* Dirty and disagreeable girl! You never cleaned your nails this morning.

JANE. She said nothing. Why didn't she explain that she could neither clean her face nor wash her hands as the water was frozen?

SCATCHERD. Hardened girl. *(She hits HELEN one last time.)* Nothing can correct your slatternly habits. *(She crosses to desk and writes* SLATTERN *on a placard which she gives to HELEN.)* You shall wear the word "slattern" for the rest of the day. *(HELEN returns to her seat, never shedding a tear, coughing slightly.)*

MILLER *(rings handbell)*. All rise.

(SCHOOLGIRLS rise. A handsome woman enters—it is MISS TEMPLE.)

MISS TEMPLE. Good morning, pupils.

GIRLS. Good morning, Miss Temple.

MISS TEMPLE. You had this morning a breakfast which you could not eat; you must be hungry;—I have ordered a lunch of bread and cheese to be served to all. *(The other TEACHERS look at her in alarm.)*

SCATCHERD. Miss Temple!

MISS TEMPLE. It is done on my responsibility. *(A tray of bread and cheese is passed among the STUDENTS.)* Monitor of the first class. Bring the globe. Second class to French. Third class to arithmetic.

SCATCHERD. Quickly! *(As the GIRLS break up into groups. MILLER points out YOUNG JANE to MISS TEMPLE.)*

MISS TEMPLE. Our new pupil, Jane Eyre?

YOUNG JANE. Yes, ma'am.

MISS TEMPLE. Is this the first time you have left your parents to come to school?

YOUNG JANE. I have no parents, ma'am.

MISS TEMPLE *(gently touching JANE's cheek)*. I hope you'll be a good child. Join the third class for arithmetic.

YOUNG JANE. Thank you, ma'am. *(As YOUNG JANE moves to her place. The bell sounds again.)*

MILLER. All rise.

(The BROCKLEHURSTS enter, MR. and MRS. and their daughter, AUGUSTA, splendidly attired in velvet, silks and furs.)

MISS TEMPLE. Good morning, Mr. Brocklehurst, Mrs. Brocklehurst, Augusta. *(They nod "good morning.")*

BROCKLEHURST. Miss Temple, the housekeeper has informed me that a lunch of bread and cheese has been served. How is this? The regulations allow for no such meal.

MISS TEMPLE. The breakfast was ill-prepared and inedible.

BROCKLEHURST. Madam, a little accidental disappointment of the appetite should not be an excuse for pampering, but a test of the spirit. The Lord himself called upon His disciples to suffer hunger and thirst for His sake. Oh, madam, when you put bread and cheese into these children's mouths, you may feed their vile bodies, but you starve their immortal souls! *(HELEN coughs and is noticed by BROCKLEHURST.)* Miss Temple—what is that girl with curled hair? Curled all over?

MISS TEMPLE. It is Helen Burns, sir.

BROCKLEHURST. Why has she curled hair in utter defiance of every principle of this house?

MISS TEMPLE. Helen Burns' hair curls naturally, sir.

BROCKLEHURST. Naturally! But we are not to conform to nature! I desire the hair to be arranged closely and modestly. Her hair must be cut off entirely. Miss Scatcherd, remove her from this room and return her to us with her hair shorn. *(SCATCHERD grabs scissors from the desk and removes HELEN from the room. YOUNG JANE, watching HELEN leave, accidentally drops her slate which breaks in two. BROCKLEHURST turns on her. She has knelt to pick up the slate.)* A careless girl! Come forward. Ah, it is the new pupil. Fetch the stool. *(A high stool is brought out.)* Place her upon it. *(YOUNG JANE is placed on the stool.)* Ladies, Miss Temple, teachers and children—you all see this girl? God has graciously given her the shape that He has given to all of us. Who would think that the Evil One has already found an agent in her? You see before you an alien in our flock. You must be on your guard against her. Scrutinize her actions and weigh well her words for this girl—this girl is—a LIAR!

MRS. BROCKLEHURST.	AUGUSTA.
How shocking!	Oh dear!

BROCKLEHURST. You will place upon her the placard "liar" for all to know it.

(He writes placard and gives it to MILLER to place on YOUNG JANE. HELEN is brought back—shorn of her locks.)

And here is our other sinner. Fetch the stool for her as well and place her upon it. They both will remain there until I see fit to dismiss them. The rest of you accompany us to the dormitories for an inspection of your rooms. You may sing the hymn "Walk With Me" to remind you of your higher calling. Follow quickly!

(MUSIC: "Walk with Me"—SCHOOLGIRLS. BROCKLEHURST sails out followed quickly by MRS. BROCK-

LEHURST and AUGUSTA. MISS TEMPLE nods to the rest to file out. As they do, singing the hymn, they look up to YOUNG JANE and HELEN with awe and admiration. The two GIRLS are now alone. YOUNG JANE bursts into tears.)

JANE. I had meant to be so good, and to do so much at Lowood: to make so many friends and to earn respect; now here I was again crushed, trodden on.

HELEN. Don't cry, little Jane.

YOUNG JANE. How can you speak to a girl the whole world believes to be a liar!

HELEN. The whole world is made up of hundreds of millions. I don't think they were all here.

YOUNG JANE. What have I to do with hundreds of millions? All who were here despise me after what Mr. Brocklehurst said.

HELEN. Mr. Brocklehurst is little liked here; he never took steps to make himself liked. Teachers and pupils may look coldly on you for a day or two, but they have friendly feelings in their hearts. Besides, Jane...

YOUNG JANE. Yes, Helen...

HELEN. If all the world hated you and believed you wicked, but your conscience approved, you would find it possible to become what you yourself would approve.

YOUNG JANE. If others don't love me, I would rather die than live.

HELEN. Hush, Jane! You think too much of the love of human beings. There is an invisible world and a kingdom of spirits who watch us and guard us. Angels who see our torture and carry us from this life into the glory beyond it.

YOUNG JANE. Is that how you bear your punishment, Helen?
HELEN. I bear it because I am deserving of it. I am careless, my mind wanders—Miss Scatcherd, who is naturally neat and punctual has a right to reprimand me.
YOUNG JANE. But to cut your beautiful hair. I could never forgive them for that.
HELEN. Love your enemies, Jane.
YOUNG JANE. That I could never do.
HELEN. Life seems to me too short to be spent in nursing animosity and registering wrongs.

(She coughs. MISS TEMPLE returns.)

MISS TEMPLE. Have you coughed much today, Helen?
HELEN. Not quite so much, Miss Temple.
MISS TEMPLE. And the pain in your chest?
HELEN. It is a little better.
MISS TEMPLE. Come down, both of you. Mr. Brocklehurst is gone. How is it with you, Jane Eyre? Have you cried your grief away?
YOUNG JANE. That I never shall do, ma'am...
MISS TEMPLE. Why?
YOUNG JANE. Because I have been wrongly accused; and now you, and everyone, will think me wicked.
MISS TEMPLE. We will think you what YOU prove yourself to be. Be a good girl and we will believe you so.
YOUNG JANE. Shall I, Miss Temple?
MISS TEMPLE. Yes, you shall. Now come along with me, both of you, I have a warm fire in my room and some seed-cake and tea. Jane, you know a criminal when accused is allowed to speak in his own defense. Come, de-

fend yourself to us now as well as you can. *(With her arms about both girls, she walks them off to her room.)*

JANE. I feasted that evening as on nectar and ambrosia as Miss Temple and Helen listened patiently to all my outpourings. No one had ever listened to me before. From that hour, I set to work afresh. I was promoted to a higher class, I learned French and drawing. For the first time in my life, I had friends.

(SCHOOLGIRLS enter and begin to rearrange the benches into beds in a sickroom.)

JANE. Then the spring came, usually a time for rejoicing, but as the earth warmed, Lowood sat in a cradle of fog and the fog bred pestilence. Typhoid transformed our classroom into a hospital.

(The weakened STUDENTS are seen. Some lying on the benches. Some bodies covered over—then carried out. A DOCTOR and the TEACHERS attend.)

JANE. Over half the girls lay ill at one time. Many went home only to die. My dearest friend, Helen Burns, like me, escaped the epidemic. Her complaint was not typhoid, but consumption.

(YOUNG JANE enters with a handful of wildflowers. She meets MISS MILLER.)

YOUNG JANE. Where is Helen? She is not in the dormitory.
MILLER. Miss Temple has had her taken to her own room.

Act I   JANE EYRE   31

YOUNG JANE. May I go and see her?
MILLER. Oh no, child! She is doing very poorly.
YOUNG JANE. Has the doctor been to see her?
MILLER. He says she'll not be here long. *(MILLER exits.)*
JANE. Nothing could keep me from my dear friend's side. As soon as I could, I slipped off my shoes and stole quietly to Miss Temple's room.

SCENE 7: MISS TEMPLE'S ROOM.

SCATCHERD *(joining MISS TEMPLE at HELEN's sickbed)*. Miss Temple, Julia Severn is delirious in the fever room.
MISS TEMPLE. I'll come. *(She joins SCATCHERD and exits. YOUNG JANE steals to HELEN's bedside with the flowers.)*
YOUNG JANE. Helen, are you awake?
HELEN *(stirs and turns to YOUNG JANE)*. Jane?
YOUNG JANE *(climbing on the bed beside her)*. I picked some flowers for you today, Helen. So many of your favorites.
HELEN. You came to bid me goodbye, then.
YOUNG JANE. Are you going home?
HELEN. Yes, to my last home.
YOUNG JANE. No, no, Helen! *(HELEN is racked with coughing. YOUNG JANE calms her.)*
HELEN. You mustn't worry, dear Jane. I am very happy. By dying young I shall escape great sufferings. I had not the qualities or talents to make my way very well in this

world. You have, Jane, for my sake will you use your talents to the utmost?

YOUNG JANE. For your sake, Helen, I will try. But, where will you go? Will the spirits take you?

HELEN. They are here with us now. They are opening a door for me to enter.

(MUSIC: Offstage the SCHOOLGIRLS sing a vespers hymn.)

YOUNG JANE. When I die, will you open that door for me?

HELEN. Yes, Jane, I will. Now, I feel as if I could sleep; but don't leave me, Jane; I like to have you near me.

YOUNG JANE *(snuggling up in HELEN's arms)*. No one will ever take me away.

HELEN. Are you warm, darling?

YOUNG JANE. Yes.

HELEN. Good night, Jane.

YOUNG JANE. Good night, Helen.

(They close their eyes. The GIRLS in the distance are finishing their hymn. HELEN's hand slowly relaxes and the flowers fall to the floor. MISS TEMPLE comes into the room and stands quietly at the head of the bed looking at the sleeping children entwined in each other's arms. She feels HELEN's forehead and realizes she is dead.)

MISS TEMPLE. God bless you, my children. *(The lights fade.)*

SCENE 8: HELEN'S GRAVE/LIMBO

(The lights come up in a separate area where JANE kneels placing flowers at a gravesite. ADULT JANE now enters the story.)

JANE. Helen's grave is in the Brockleridge churchyard. I tended it and kept it with flowers for the nine years I remained at Lowood. Six as a student and three as a teacher. My dearest friend and companion became Maria Temple. I learned much from her—to quiet my passions and to be content. It was quite a blow to me when she decided to leave Lowood to be married.

(MISS TEMPLE approaches JANE.)

MISS TEMPLE. Will you have this from me, as remembrance of our friendship? *(She hands JANE her gold watch. They embrace.)*
JANE. I cannot stay on here now. It will be empty here. The only thing I am suitable for is service and I am ready to serve as a teacher or governess.
MISS TEMPLE. Place an advertisement. I will procure glowing references for you. Jane, you are ready for life's adventure. *(MISS TEMPLE exits.)*
JANE *(stepping forward into a pool of light)*. "A young lady is desirous of a situation in a private family where the children are under fourteen. She is qualified to teach good English, French, Drawing, Arithmetic and Music. Respond to Jane Eyre, Lowood School."

(Lights up on MRS. FAIRFAX.)

MRS. FAIRFAX. "If Jane Eyre is in a position to give satisfactory references, a situation can be offered her where there is but one pupil, a little girl; the salary is thirty pounds per year. Send all references to Mrs. Fairfax, Thornfield Hall." *(Lights out.)*
JANE. That was my only acceptance.

(She walks to an area of light containing MR. BROCKLEHURST.)

JANE. Mr. Brocklehurst, I wish to tender my resignation. I have acquired the position of governess for a Mrs. Fairfax at Thornfield Hall.
BROCKLEHURST. Your guardian, Mrs. Reed, must be written to.
JANE. She was.

(MRS. REED appears in a pool of light.)

MRS. REED. Jane Eyre might do as she pleases. I, long ago, relinquished all interference in her affairs. *(Light out on REED and BROCKLEHURST.)*
JANE. On the day I was packed and ready to depart I received a surprise visitor. My only visitor in nine years at Lowood.

(BESSIE enters and rushes to JANE.)

BESSIE. Jane Eyre, I'm sure! I could have told her anywhere! Come, you've not quite forgotten me, Miss Jane?
JANE. Bessie? Bessie! *(They embrace.)*

BESSIE. When I heard you was going to another part of the country, I thought I'd just set-off. I've long wanted to see you, whether your relations did or not.

JANE. What of them, Bessie?

BESSIE. Master John never made out in college. He's quite dissipated and spends a great deal of money which causes many arguments with his mother.

JANE. How is Eliza?

BESSIE. Eliza is as miserly as ever. She manages the estate. We actually have to buy the eggs from her. Georgiana is quite the plump little beauty. She almost eloped with a young lord, but Eliza told her mother and her mother put a stop to that.

JANE. Oh, dear!

BESSIE. But, Miss Jane, did you ever hear from your father's kinsfolk?

JANE. Never.

BESSIE. Well, a few years ago a Mr. Eyre came to Gateshead. Quite the gentleman. Not at all the poor relation Missus had said. He was looking for you. Missus was quite high with him—said "She's away to school"—well, Mr. Eyre was very disappointed because he was sailing immediately for an island and couldn't see you.

JANE. What island, Bessie?

BESSIE. It was thousands of miles off—they make wine there—

JANE. I heard Mrs. Reed mention an island once—was it—Madeira?

BESSIE. Yes, that is it—Madeira.

(MISS MILLER enters with some SCHOOLGIRLS.)

MISS MILLER. The coach is here, Miss Jane.
JANE. Oh, thank you, Miss Miller. Bessie, thank you for coming to see me!

BESSIE.	MISS MILLER & GIRLS.
Good luck in your new situation.	Safe journey, Miss Jane!

(MUSIC: Journey to Thornfield. As JANE speaks, BESSIE and MISS MILLER recede and THORNFIELD assembles around JANE.)

JANE. My sixteen-hour journey by coach began as a charming adventure, but as I neared my destination the throb of fear became predominant—what would I find at Thornfield? It is a very strange sensation to inexperienced youth to feel itself quite alone in the world, cut adrift from every connection. We passed through the manufacturing town of Millcote and then after several miles, approached a great park ringed with mighty old thorn trees—home to a rookery whose cawing tenants were on the wing as the carriage approached the grand manor-house. *(The sound of rooks. JANE turns—she is in:)*

SCENE 9: THORNFIELD

(MRS. FAIRFAX appears carrying a lantern. She is an elderly lady. Following her are the servants, JOHN, who is about her age, and LEAH, quite young.)

MRS. FAIRFAX. Ah, Miss Eyre?

JANE. Mrs. Fairfax, I suppose?

MRS. FAIRFAX. How do you do, my dear. I am afraid you've had a tedious ride; you must be cold, come to the fire. Leah, tell the cook Miss Jane has arrived and she may serve the dinner. John, carry Miss Jane's luggage to the room prepared for her. *(They bow, curtsy and exit.)*

JANE. Shall I have the pleasure of seeing Miss Fairfax this evening?

MRS. FAIRFAX. Miss Fairfax?

JANE. My pupil.

MRS. FAIRFAX. Oh, you mean Miss Varens.

JANE. She is not your daughter?

MRS. FAIRFAX. Oh dear, no. I have no family. She is Mr. Rochester's ward.

JANE. Mr. Rochester?

MRS. FAIRFAX. The owner of Thornfield.

JANE. I thought Thornfield belonged to you.

MRS. FAIRFAX. To me? Bless you, child; what an idea! I am only the housekeeper. Mr. Rochester is seldom at home. But, it will be quite pleasant with you here. Ah, here comes your little charge now.

(ADELE runs in. She is very pretty with a redundancy of hair falling to her waist. She speaks only in French.)

ADELE. *C'est là ma gouvernante?*

MRS. FAIRFAX. Miss Adela, this is the lady who is to teach you and make you a clever woman some day.

ADELE. *Bon soir, mademoiselle. Qu'est-ce que vous nom?*

JANE. Eyre—Jane Eyre.

ADELE. *Aire? Bah! C'est tres difficile.*

MRS. FAIRFAX. I hope you can understand her, for I can't make it out.

ADELE. *Aire?*

MRS. FAIRFAX. Her mother was on the continent. Perhaps you can find out more about her.

JANE. *Adele, ou est votre mere?*

ADELE. *Mama a va au ciel. Elle habite avec la Vierge Marie. Mais, allez-vous avec moi! Mesdames, vous etes servies! J'ai bien faim, moi!* (*She skips off in the direction of the dining room.*)

MRS. FAIRFAX. That much I understand, for she is always hungry. Come, Miss Eyre—(*A sudden strange and chilling laugh is heard. It is not mirthful, but full of terrifying menace.*)

JANE. Mrs. Fairfax? Did you hear that?

MRS. FAIRFAX. Some of the servants, very likely—perhaps Grace Poole. I often hear her; she sews in one of the rooms on the third floor. (*The laugh sounds again.*) Grace Poole?

(*From a doorway suspended way up in the air, a large mannish figure of a WOMAN appears. Square-set, red-haired.*)

MRS. FAIRFAX. Too much noise, Grace. Remember directions! (*GRACE POOLE curtsies and disappears.*)

(*ADELE runs on impatiently, then runs off.*)

ADELE. *Mesdames!*
MRS. FAIRFAX. Coming, Adele! Come along, Miss Eyre.

(She bustles off. JANE remains quietly thoughtful, then turns to the AUDIENCE, donning a hat, bonnet and shawl—the lights fade.)

JANE. We spent the winter together quite cozily, but I hope I will not be blamed for being what some might call discontented. I could not help it. Women feel just as men feel and it is narrow-minded to say we ought to confine ourselves to making puddings and knitting stockings. This restlessness often took me on extended walks from Thornfield to Millcote and it was on such a walk that all life changed. I was returning from town along a narrow lane bounded by hedges. It was very dark.

(MUSIC: A galloping horse is heard approaching.)

JANE. I heard a horse approaching, suddenly a great dog was beside me. *(A large dog's bark. It continues.)* I jumped into the middle of the lane directly in front of the horse! *(A horse neighs and comes to a stop. Blackout. We hear shouting from offstage. JANE is gone.)*

ROCHESTER'S VOICE. Mrs. Fairfax! John! Leah! Come to me directly! John!

(The SERVANTS, carrying lights, run through the hall and out the front door. MRS. FAIRFAX follows.)

MRS. FAIRFAX *(from the door)*. Oh, sir. What has happened?
ROCHESTER'S VOICE. The horse fell on some ice. We came upon a stranger on the road and down we went.

Send for the surgeon—I have a bad sprain, though I daresay nothing is broken.

(EDWARD ROCHESTER appears supported by JOHN and LEAH. He is enveloped in a riding cloak, fur-collared and steel clasped. A broad, big man with stern features and a heavy brow. His large Newfoundland, PILOT, is heard barking the alarm outside.)

MRS. FAIRFAX. John, place Mr. Rochester by the fire, then hurry for the doctor. Leah, tell cook to prepare some hot tea and soup. Are you very hungry, sir?

ROCHESTER *(as he is being carried off)*. No, that will be fine. But, Pilot will eat all of you, if he is not soon fed.

MRS. FAIRFAX. Leah, have cook set out Pilot's dish at once. *(Calling out door as barking becomes vehement.)* Just a moment, Pilot. Oh! Pilot!

(She closes the door quickly as JANE returns by the back way.)

MRS. FAIRFAX. Miss Jane, the master has returned and met with a horrible accident. It seems someone accosted him on the lane and toppled his horse.

JANE. On Hay Lane, just now?

MRS. FAIRFAX. Just now. At any rate, fetch Adele, he'll wish to see her and you. You might want a brooch and a little combing of the hair. I must see to Mr. Rochester.

(MRS. FAIRFAX hurries off. ADELE, beside herself with excitement, rushes to meet JANE, who is trying to improve her own appearance.)

ADELE. *Oh, mademoiselle, mon ami Monsieur de Rochester est arrivé! Et cela doit signifier qu'il y aura la'-dedans un cadeau pour moi. Une boite! Oo la la! Ma boite!*
JANE. Adele, *silence, maintenant.* Remember your manners, *s'il vous plait.*

SCENE 10: THE LIBRARY

(A roaring fire and MR. ROCHESTER stretched out on a sofa in front of it. MRS. FAIRFAX ushers them in.)

MRS. FAIRFAX. Ah, sir, here is Adele.
ADELE. *Ah, mon ami, monsieur, je suis heureuse de vous voir!*
ROCHESTER. Carefully, Adele, you must mind my foot—it is very sore and you will make it worse if you jump on it. Down, Adele! You're worse than Pilot.
MRS. FAIRFAX. And here is Miss Eyre, sir.
ROCHESTER *(without looking as JANE seats herself quite a distance away).* Let Miss Eyre be seated.
ADELE. *N'est-ce pas, monsieur, qu'il y a un cadeau pour mademoiselle?*
ROCHESTER. Who talks of *cadeaux*? Does Miss Eyre expect *un cadeau*? Where the deuce is she? Who is that sitting in the shadows—come forward. *(Reluctantly, JANE does.)*
ADELE *(running to her and pulling her forward).* *C'est la ma gouvernante!*
ROCHESTER. Oh ho! Oh ho ho! So this is Miss Eyre.

ADELE. *Oui, monsieur.* Miss Ayre! *Avez-vous une boite pour mademoiselle?*

ROCHESTER. Do you expect a gift, Miss Eyre?

JANE. I hardly know, sir; I have little experience of them.

ROCHESTER. Well, you are not so unsophisticated as Adele who demands a *cadeau* the moment she sees me. Adele, *voyez-vous derriere mon divan.*

ADELE *(drags a large box from behind the sofa—squealing).* Ma boite! Ma boite!

ROCHESTER. Yes, there is your *boite* at last. Mrs. Fairfax, take Adele to the other side of the room and help her disembowel her *boite!* It will be one of the most benevolent acts you've ever performed.

MRS. FAIRFAX. Come along, Adele.

ROCHESTER. Adele, *tiens-toi tranquille, enfant. Comprends-tu?*

ADELE. *Oui, monsieur.*

ROCHESTER. *Merci!* (MRS. FAIRFAX *removes* ADELE *to a far corner to open her large box.)* Miss Eyre, would you be so kind as to pour me a cup of tea? Careful not to spill it, I've suffered enough accidents at your hands for one day. *(JANE attempts to speak, when ADELE squeals.)*

ADELE *(pulling out a lovely hat).* Oh, *ciel!*

ROCHESTER. Adele!

ADELE. *Pardon, mon cher, monsieur. Pardon.* (MRS. FAIRFAX *takes* ADELE *off.)*

ROCHESTER. You have been resident in my house three months, where did you come from?

JANE. Lowood School, sir.

ROCHESTER. How long were you there?

JANE. Nine years, sir.

ROCHESTER. I thought half so much time in that place would have done anyone in. But, then, perhaps you are of another world, bewitching and spooking horses with your fairy charms?

JANE *(as she hands him his tea).* I am quite of this world, sir, I assure you.

ROCHESTER. Resume your seat! I do not prefer the society of simple-minded old ladies and lisping brats. Draw your chair closer! If you please, that is! Confound these civilities—do you agree with me that I have the right to be a little masterful—I'm almost old enough to be your father and have roamed over half the globe while you have lived quietly.

JANE. I don't think, sir, you have the right to command me, merely because you are older or have seen more of the world. Your claim to superiority depends on the use you have made of your time and experience.

ROCHESTER. Promptly spoken. Lord knows time has knocked me about; experience kneaded me with her knuckles until I'm hard and tough as an India-rubber ball. But, will you receive my orders without being hurt by my tone of command?

JANE. You seem to forget you pay me thirty pounds per year to receive your orders, sir. But, since you did forget and are kind enough to care whether a dependent is comfortable, I agree heartily.

ROCHESTER. I mentally shake hands with you for your answer. Not three in three thousand raw school-girl governesses would have answered just now as you have done. However, you may have intolerable defects to counter-balance your few good points.

JANE. And so may you.

ROCHESTER. Oh, I have plenty of faults of my own. Though some of my faults fate forced upon me; and I degenerated badly, though I could reform—if... But, I have the right to get pleasure out of life; and I will get it cost what it may. *(He stirs violently and winces from pain.)*

JANE. Sir, perhaps we should retire, so that you can rest.

ROCHESTER. No, no, a while longer till the doctor has come. Bear with me. Besides, Adele is now undergoing the robing process. Coquetry runs in her blood, blends with her brains and seasons the marrow of her bones. So—where was I?

JANE. Degenerating, sir.

ROCHESTER *(amused)*. Ah, yes. But, why should I if I can get sweet, fresh pleasure as wild as the honey the bee gathers on the moor.

JANE. It may sting or taste bitter, sir.

ROCHESTER. How do you know—you never tried it.

JANE. Sir, a dear friend once said to me that if you tried hard, you would in time find it possible to become what you yourself would approve.

ROCHESTER. Justly thought, Miss Eyre, but at this moment I am paving the road to hell with energy. *(JANE rises.)* Where are you going?

JANE. I should go to Adele.

ROCHESTER. You are afraid of me, because I talk like a Sphynx.

JANE. Though I am bewildered, I am certainly not afraid.

ROCHESTER. You ARE afraid—your self-love dreads making a blunder.

JANE. In that sense, yes—I have no wish to talk nonsense.

ROCHESTER. But, if you did, it would be in such a grave manner, that I should mistake it for sense. Do you never laugh, Miss Eyre? You look puzzled and you study me. Do you find me handsome?

JANE. No, sir.

ROCHESTER. Ah, and though you are not pretty any more than I am handsome, your puzzled look becomes you.

(MRS. FAIRFAX returns with ADELE, who is now wearing her new dress.)

ROCHESTER. As I predicted, a miniature Celine Varens!

ADELE. *Est-ce que ma robe va bien? Et mes souliers? Et mes bas? Tenez, je crois que je vais danser! (ADELE twirls about the room, dancing to her music box.)*

ROCHESTER. She is her mother's daughter. I am not the father, as you may have suspected, but I once cherished a *"grande passion"* for her mother. And ugly as I was, I thought myself her idol, I installed her in a hotel, servants, carriages, diamonds, until I happened to call one evening when Celine did not expect me. You never felt jealousy, did you, Miss Eyre? Of course not; because you've never felt love. You have both sentiments yet to experience.

ADELE *(finishing her dance, runs to him). Monsieur, je vous remercie mille fois de votre bonté.*

ROCHESTER. What are you about, Miss Eyre, to let Adele stay up so long? Take her to bed! Draw the curtains, Mrs. Fairfax—I will sleep here tonight. If the doctor should ever arrive, show him in. Now, good night!

(The three curtsy and leave him, MRS. FAIRFAX drawing the curtain.)

MRS. FAIRFAX. Miss Eyre, would you be so kind as to wait for the doctor. I will take Adele up to bed.

JANE. Mr. Rochester is very changeable and abrupt.

MRS. FAIRFAX. Perhaps, I never think of it. But allowance should be made.

JANE. Why?

MRS. FAIRFAX. Family troubles. His father always preferred his older brother and left all his money to him. Mr. Rochester tried every way he could to please his father—every way he could. He went off to the West Indies and only returned when his brother had died without a will and the estate came back to him. Though, now, he shuns this old place.

JANE. Why should he shun it?

MRS. FAIRFAX *(evasive)*. Perhaps he thinks it gloomy. Come, Adele.

JANE *(to AUDIENCE)*. I waited and saw the doctor in. He pronounced that it was indeed a sprain, and I'm sure quite a painful one, for Mr. Rochester was given a strong sleeping sedative. I could not sleep, blood was pounding through my veins. With Mr. Rochester the blanks of my existence were suddenly filled up. His presence in the room was more cheering than the brightest fire. Yes, he was proud, sardonic, moody, but I believed this had its source in some cruel cross of fate. I grieved for his grief and would have given anything to assuage it. *(JANE is startled by a demonic laugh—low, suppressed and deep—coming from somewhere without.)* Who is there? Grace Poole, is that you?

Act I   JANE EYRE   47

(The laugh is heard again. JANE rises, takes a candle and ventures forth. Immediately, she breathes in smoke which is coming from where MR. ROCHESTER sleeps. She throws back the drape. Flames are rising up around the sofa.)

JANE. Wake! Wake! Sir, you must wake! Dear God, he's senseless. *(She hurls flowers from a vase and throws the water on ROCHESTER.)*

ROCHESTER *(groggily)*. Is there a flood?

JANE. No sir, there's a fire!

ROCHESTER *(as they both beat out the fire, pull down draperies)*. Good God, is that Jane Eyre? Have you plotted to drown me?

JANE. Somebody has plotted something. Shall I call Mrs. Fairfax?

ROCHESTER. No. What can she do? Let her sleep.

JANE. Then Leah and John...

ROCHESTER. No, no Just be still. Hand me that dressing gown—since you've decided to give me a bath! *(ROCHESTER strips off his wet clothes, JANE approaches modestly.)* Turn about, if you please. *(JANE hands him the dressing gown. Supporting himself behind a large armchair, he puts it on.)* Did you see anyone or anything?

JANE. No, sir. I heard an odd laugh and look, sir, here is a candlestick. There is a woman who sews on the third floor who laughs in that way—Grace Poole.

ROCHESTER. Just so. Grace Poole—you have guessed it. She is an odd person, as you say. I will have to deal with her. You are no talking fool; say nothing about it. I will account for all this; now return to your room, I shall do very well, here in this armchair for the remainder of the night.

JANE. Good night, then, sir.

ROCHESTER. Are you quitting me so quickly?

JANE. You said I might go, sir.

ROCHESTER. Not without a word or two of acknowledgment—why, you have saved my life! You walk past me as if we were strangers! At least shake hands. *(He holds out his hand, she takes it. He holds hers in both his hands.)* I have the pleasure in owing you an immense debt. I cannot say more.

JANE. Good night, sir. There is no debt owed in any case.

ROCHESTER *(still holding her hand)*. I knew, Jane, you would do me good; I saw it in your eyes when I first beheld you.

JANE. But, I had caused your horse to fall, sir.

ROCHESTER. Fairies and sprights cause all sorts of things to topple—but, ah,—well, my cherished preserver, good night. *(He still holds her hand.)*

JANE. I'm glad I happened to be awake. *(She attempts to go and he abruptly drops her hand.)*

ROCHESTER. Well, leave me, then. Draw the curtain. *(She does. He is gone.)*

JANE *(to AUDIENCE)*. I never thought of sleep that night. I rose as soon as day dawned, both wishing and fearing to see Mr. Rochester.

(MRS. FAIRFAX enters as lights come up.)

MRS. FAIRFAX. Jane, a terrible thing happened in the night. An ember from the fire jumped onto the drapes by Mr. Rochester—oh—luckily he was able to put the fire out.

JANE. Where is Mr. Rochester?
MRS. FAIRFAX. He is gone. Took the carriage. Won't be back for several days.

(LEAH and JOHN pass with damaged drapery.)

MRS. FAIRFAX. Dispose of those and then come back to help me clean the room. Miss Eyre, please keep Adele away from here until all is repaired.

(JANE is left alone. GRACE POOLE slowly emerges out of the darkness and startles JANE.)

JANE. Good morning, Grace. Did you hear what happened here last night?
GRACE POOLE. Only master fell asleep before the fire was out.
JANE. Did Mr. Rochester wake nobody?
GRACE POOLE. The servants sleep so far away they would not be likely to hear; your room was the nearest, perhaps you heard a noise?
JANE. I did. At first I thought it was Pilot, but dogs cannot laugh; and I am certain I heard a laugh.
GRACE POOLE. It is hardly likely the master would laugh, miss, you must have been dreaming.
JANE. I was not dreaming.

(MRS. FAIRFAX returns with a bolt of fabric.)

MRS. FAIRFAX. Grace, you'll be needed to sew new drapes for the library—

GRACE POOLE *(taking the fabric).* Yes, ma'am. *(During the following, GRACE makes the long ascent to her room on the third floor.)*

MRS. FAIRFAX. We must have all repaired on Mr. Rochester's return. He has left strict instructions. There will be a large house party. He expressly said that you must bring Adele to join the festivities every evening.

JANE. A large party?

MRS. FAIRFAX. Yes, the ladies from the Leas and their friends.

JANE. Ladies?

MRS. FAIRFAX. Oh yes, and the belle of the whole county will be here—she's a beauty—I believe Mr. Rochester quite fancies her—Miss Blanche Ingram.

(GRACE has reached her door, when she opens it a laugh is heard. She closes the door quickly. Blackout.)

SCENE 11: THE MUSIC ROOM and PARLOR

(MUSIC: Piano—an early 19th-century ballade. The party is in progress. MR. ROCHESTER is playing for the dark and beautiful BLANCHE INGRAM dressed in a white gown, with an amber scarf over one shoulder and tied at the waist. She is entertaining her friends: AMY and LOUISA ESHTON, SIR GEORGE and LADY LYNN and their sons, HENRY and FREDERICK LYNN. Her mother, the DOWAGER LADY INGRAM, wears a crimson velvet robe and a shawl-turban of golden India fabric which lends her an imperial dignity. Her other

daughter, MARY INGRAM, is also straight and tall as a poplar, but lacks the vivacity of her remarkable sister. JOHN and LEAH under MRS. FAIRFAX's direction prepare the drawing room. JANE enters with ADELE, giving her last-minute instructions.)

ADELE. *Est-ce que je ne puis pas prendre une seule de ces fleurs, mademoiselle? Seulement pour completer ma toilette.*

JANE *(breaking off a rose from one of the arrangements and pinning it on ADELE).* You think too much of your *toilette*, Adele, but you may have a flower. *(The MUSIC finishes.)*

ADELE. *Oh, ils vient!*

(JANE sits in an out of the way corner doing needlework. The LADIES arrive followed by the GENTLEMEN. ADELE runs forward and curtsies.)

ADELE. *Bonjour, mesdames.*

BLANCHE. Oh, dear, what a little puppet!

LADY LYNN. It is Mr. Rochester's ward, I suppose—the little French girl he was speaking of.

LOUISA. What a love of a child.

AMY. Come, sit with us, dear. *(LOUISA and AMY sit ADELE between them on a sofa.)*

LADY INGRAM. Mr. Rochester, I thought you were not fond of children?

ROCHESTER *(walks with a cane).* Nor am I.

LADY INGRAM. What induced you to take charge of such a little moppet as that?

BLANCHE. Where DID you pick her up?

ROCHESTER. I did not pick her up, she was left on my hands.

BLANCHE. You should have sent her to school.

ROCHESTER. She has a governess.

BLANCHE. Oh, yes, I believe I saw her hiding in the corner, ah, there she is! You should hear mama on the subject of governesses: Mary and I had at least a dozen, all of them *incubi*; half of them detestable, the rest ridiculous.

LADY INGRAM. My dearest, don't mention governesses; I have suffered a martyrdom with their excesses and caprices. You know, if a woman cannot marry, or lacks the charms to succeed at anything else, she becomes a governess. I thank heaven I have done with them.

LADY LYNN. Careful, she might hear you.

LADY INGRAM. *Tant pis!* I hope it may do her good!

HENRY LYNN. Rochester, you promised charades after music. When do we begin?

ROCHESTER. Ah, yes. Take the lights into the ballroom—chairs have been placed for us there. Adele, you will say good night—you've seen your lovely ladies.

ADELE. *Au revoir, mesdames, messieurs. (JANE rises to accompany ADELE.)*

ROCHESTER. Mrs. Fairfax, you'll take her up, won't you? *(Everyone notices this as JANE resumes her seat.)* Charades! Let us choose up sides. Henry and I will be captains. Miss Ingram is mine, of course.

HENRY. Miss Amy...

ROCHESTER. ...and Miss Louisa.

HENRY. Miss Mary.

ROCHESTER. Lady Lynn, thank you.

HENRY. Lady Ingram.

LADY INGRAM. Oh, I really think I should sit it out.
HENRY. Frederick, then.
ROCHESTER. Sir George.
ALL GUESTS. Sir George! *(SIR GEORGE is hard of hearing.)*
HENRY. Ah, but we're one short. *(Looking to JANE.)* Will you play?
BLANCHE. She looks too stupid for any game.
LADY INGRAM. I will complete your side, if you are short.
HENRY. Ever the saving grace, good Lady Ingram. Off we go. *(They pick up lights and exit to the ballroom. ROCHESTER lingers, alone with JANE.)*
ROCHESTER. Will you come and watch?
JANE. No, I am tired, sir.
ROCHESTER. What is the matter?
JANE. Nothing at all, sir.
ROCHESTER. Did you take any cold the night you half-drowned me?
JANE. Not the least.
ROCHESTER. You're a little depressed—what about? Tell me.
JANE. Nothing—nothing, sir.
ROCHESTER. I affirm that you are: so much so that I see a few more words will bring tears to your eyes—indeed, there they are now, shining and swimming; if I had time, I would know what all this means.

(BLANCHE returns.)

BLANCHE. Edward, how are we to start without you?

ROCHESTER. Ah, yes. I'm coming. *(He starts off. BLANCHE exits ahead of him. He turns back to JANE.)* Jane—ah—as long as the guests stay, I expect you in the drawing room every evening. I'll excuse you this once, my little...

BLANCHE *(off)*. Edward!

ROCHESTER. Well, good night. *(He goes.)*

JANE *(to AUDIENCE)*. I had not intended to love him. Yet, while I breathe and think I must love him. I could see that he was going to marry Blanche Ingram, for family, for political reasons, but not because he had given his heart to her...not to her. The party continued for a week; one afternoon, Mr. Rochester and the men were out and the ladies received two unusual visitors.

(The LADIES have assembled for the day and amuse themselves at various diversions. The servant, JOHN, addresses them.)

JOHN. Pardon, ladies, but there is an old gypsy woman come to the back door who will not be persuaded to go away.

LADY INGRAM. What on earth does she want?

JOHN. To tell the unmarried ladies here their fortunes.

LADY INGRAM. Dear Lord.

AMY. What is she like?

JOHN. A shocking ugly creature to be sure.

LOUISA. Oh, let's have her in.

LADY INGRAM. I cannot possibly condone such a thing.

BLANCHE. Indeed, mama, you must and will. I have a curiosity to have my fortune told. *(The young LADIES add their approvals, as BLANCHE turns haughtily to*

JOHN.) Go! Show her into the library, we'll see her one by one. I mean to have her all to myself. I will go first. *(BLANCHE sails off into the library.)*

JANE *(as the time passes).* The minutes passed very slowly before the library door opened again and Miss Ingram returned.

(BLANCHE enters.)

AMY. Well, Blanche?

MARY. What did she say, sister?

LOUISA. Is she a real fortuneteller?

BLANCHE *(quite miffed).* Don't press upon me. The creature is merely a stupid, gypsy vagabond.

LOUISA. Oooo, she must have told you something awful.

BLANCHE. Go see for yourself. *(BLANCHE sits down firmly on a sofa and opens a book.)*

MARY. Oh, I can't face her alone.

AMY. Nor I.

LOUISA. John, enquire if she will see us, all three, at once. *(He goes out.)*

LADY LYNN. I wonder when the men will return?

ADELE *(who has been gazing out the window, cries out).* Voila Monsieur Rochester, *qui revient!*

BLANCHE *(runs to the window, pushing ADELE aside).* That is not Mr. Rochester's carriage! Provoking! You tiresome monkey! Who perched you at the window to give false intelligence.

(She gives an angry look toward JANE and resumes her seat. MRS. FAIRFAX comes to look out, as JOHN returns.)

JOHN. The gypsy woman says she'll take all three at once.
AMY. Oh my, all right, then. Come along. *(The three hold hands and go off.)*
MRS. FAIRFAX. John, a stranger has just arrived. Please be so kind as to let him in. *(JOHN goes off.)* I do not recognize this gentleman, I am sure.

(JOHN ushers in RICHARD MASON.)

JOHN. Mr. Richard Mason.
MASON. Please forgive the intrusion, it appears that I have come at an importune time when my friend, Mr. Rochester, is from home.
LADY INGRAM. We expect he will return shortly, Mr. Mason, with the other gentlemen of our party. Where do you come from, sir?
MASON. A long journey, ma'am. The West Indies. That is where I knew Mr. Rochester. He always disliked the heat there, the hurricanes, the rainy season. I daresay, he is much happier now. If I could trouble you for a room to lie down in till he returns?
MRS. FAIRFAX. This way, sir.

(A giggling and squealing is heard from the GIRLS off. Then they return excitedly to the room.)

LADY INGRAM. Really! The girls are having their fortunes told.
BLANCHE. By an old witch!
MASON *(somewhat alarmed)*. A witch?
BLANCHE. A fake, sir, a silly old fake.
AMY. She told us such things!

LOUISA. She knew all about us—oh, it was so exciting!
MARY. She divined our very thoughts.
BLANCHE. Really! John, give her something and send her away.
JOHN. Excuse me, ma'am, but the gypsy declares that there is yet another single lady in the room and will not go until she has seen her.
BLANCHE. What?
JOHN. Miss Eyre, I believe.
JANE. I will go, by all means. *(ALL stare at her shocked, as she walks out of the room.)*

SCENE 12: THE LIBRARY

(MUSIC: A slow gypsy tune. We now see the GYPSY for the first time—sitting in the armchair in a red cloak and broad-brimmed hat. She is gazing into the fire.)

JANE. I must warn you, I have no faith.
GYPSY. Just like your impudence, I heard it in your step as you crossed the threshhold. Why don't you tremble?
JANE. I'm not cold.
GYPSY. Why don't you turn pale?
JANE. I'm not sick.
GYPSY. Why don't you consult my art?
JANE. I'm not silly.
GYPSY *(snickering to herself)*. You are cold; you are sick; you are silly.
JANE. Prove it.

GYPSY. You are cold, because you are alone. You are sick because the sweetest feeling given to man keeps far away from you. You are silly, because you will not beckon it to approach.

JANE. You might say that to any solitary dependent in a great house.

GYPSY. What thoughts are busy in your heart while you listen to all the fine people gossiping of courtship and marriage? Have you no secret hope of your own? Do you not observe any face in particular?

JANE. I enjoy studying all the faces.

GYPSY. The face of one of the gentlemen?

JANE. I barely know the gentlemen here.

GYPSY. What of the master of the house?

JANE. What has Mr. Rochester to do with this?

GYPSY. He owes you an immense debt, does he not?

JANE. How do you know this? Has one of the servants said something?

GYPSY. You think it is because of my friend, Grace Poole.

JANE *(jumping up)*. Grace Poole! So, you are confederate with her!

GYPSY. Don't worry about her, she is not what you think she is. You say nothing of the beautiful Miss Ingram. She is to wed shortly with your master.

JANE. Shortly?

GYPSY. But I just told her something on that point which made the corners of her mouth fall half an inch.

JANE. I did not come to hear Miss Ingram's fortune, but my own.

GYPSY. Your fortune is yet doubtful, it is up to you to stretch out your hand and take up your own bliss. Your mind says "I can live alone," but what does your heart say? Will you listen to it? Rise now, Miss Eyre, and leave me—the play is played out. Shake hands first, before you go. *(JANE starts at the outstretched hand. There is a ring on the small finger which she has seen before.)*

JANE. What is this ring?

GYPSY. Well, Jane, do you know me now? *(Throws off cloak—it is ROCHESTER.)*

JANE. Sir?

ROCHESTER *(trying to undo bonnet)*. The string is in a knot—help me. Do you forgive me, Jane?

JANE. You are the one who reads minds, sir.

ROCHESTER. Rather well carried out, don't you think?

JANE. No. In short I believe you have been trying to draw me out—or in. You have been talking nonsense to make me talk nonsense.

ROCHESTER. Do you forgive me, Jane?

JANE. I cannot tell until I have thought it over. *(She starts to leave.)*

ROCHESTER *(catching her)*. Stay a moment. Tell me what the others said about the gypsy.

JANE. The others—oh! Are you aware, sir, that a stranger has arrived to see you?

ROCHESTER. A stranger—did he give his name?

(MASON is seen with a lantern—searching for a room.)

JANE. He comes from the West Indies.

ROCHESTER. The West Indies?

JANE. A Richard Mason.

ROCHESTER *(suddenly buckles, and sinks down on a bench)*. Mason!

JANE. Are you ill, sir?

ROCHESTER. Jane, I've got a blow; a blow, Jane.

JANE. Lean on me, sir.

ROCHESTER. My little friend, I wish I were on a quiet island with only you; and hideous recollections removed from me.

JANE. I'd give my life to serve you, sir.

ROCHESTER. I know that, Jane. Look in—tell me what they are all doing?

(JANE looks off—meanwhile, MASON nears GRACE POOLE's room.)

JANE. They are all laughing and talking, sir.

ROCHESTER. They don't look as though they have heard something strange?

JANE. No, sir.

ROCHESTER. Where is Mason now?

JANE. He was taken up to one of the rooms.

ROCHESTER. Go, quickly. Do not let the others know I'm here.

SCENE 13: THE HALL and LIMBO

(JANE heads for the drawing room as MASON enters POOLE's room. All the while the guests in the drawing room have been chattering gaily. The MUSIC builds as ROCHESTER approaches POOLE's door and there is an agonizing scream from within. The talking ceases, people run out toward the noise.)

BLANCHE. What is it? Who cried out?

(ROCHESTER appears above.)

ROCHESTER. Here! Here! Be composed all of you.
BLANCHE. Edward! What horror has taken place, let us know the worst?
ROCHESTER. Much ado about nothing. I startled a servant who was dozing, I'm afraid she thought me an apparition out of some nightmare. I hope I don't have that effect on everyone. *(He chuckles, others join in.)* All's well. Mrs. Fairfax, you must speak to servants who doze on the job. Please see the guests in to dinner and I will change and join you directly. Miss Ingram, I know you will aid in calming the others. *(With much chattering and relief they go off into the dining room. JANE, last, is stopped by ROCHESTER.)* Quickly, Jane, fetch me a wet sponge and the smelling salts. You don't turn sick at the sight of blood do you? Hand him out, Grace. Lock the door, do you hear me, Grace? Lock it!

(MASON is passed through the door to him. He is slumped over. His shirt bloody. JANE rushes back and they meet on the landing.)

ROCHESTER. Quickly, Jane, administer the salts. *(She does, while he tears open the shirt. There is a wide gash on MASON's upper arm. He sponges it quickly, then ties up the wound.)*
MASON. She bit me. Like a tigress. She bit me.
ROCHESTER. I warned you.
MASON. She sucked the blood. She said she'd drain my heart.
ROCHESTER. Be silent, Richard.

MASON. I'll never forget this night.

ROCHESTER. You will when you are far away from this place and back on the islands. Jane, run and tell John to come. *(She does.)* Try to stay on your feet, man. I will send you to the doctor in Millcote, then the sooner you are back at sea the better.

MASON. Rochester—let her be taken care of; let her be treated as tenderly as may be—

ROCHESTER. I do my best. Come, man—walk.

(JANE and JOHN return. They help MASON on with his coat.)

ROCHESTER. John, drive Mason to Doctor Carter, wait for him and he will direct you from there. Hurry! *(JOHN and MASON exit.)* Jane, I stand on a crater-crust that may crack and spew fire at any moment. One careless thought, one word and I'll be deprived forever of any happiness.

JANE. You are safe with me, sir.

ROCHESTER. Am I? *(He hurriedly exits.)*

JANE *(to AUDIENCE).* Life is full of strange surprises and messages.

(Pool of light up on BESSIE.)

BESSIE. "Dear Miss Jane: I am sorry to be the bearer of bad news, but I felt you should know the circumstances. Mr. John Reed died a week ago, his life had been wild and he ruined his health and the estate. They say he killed himself. Mrs. Reed, upon receiving the news, suffered a stroke. For three days she could not speak, but kept making signs. Yesterday she said your name: she said 'Bring Jane Eyre—I want to speak to her.' Mrs. Reed may be not be in her right mind, but she says your name over and over. I thought you should know. Your servant, Bessie." *(Lights out on BESSIE.)*

JANE. I prepared immediately to depart for Gateshead. I found Mr. Rochester in the music room.

SCENE 14: THE MUSIC ROOM

(The house party continues. ROCHESTER once again accompanies BLANCHE's singing. JANE walks up to the piano. BLANCHE stops in a huff and exasperatedly looks at ROCHESTER.)

BLANCHE. This person wants you.
ROCHESTER. Well, Jane.
JANE. If you please, sir, I want a leave of absence.
ROCHESTER. What to do?
JANE. My aunt is very ill.
ROCHESTER. The deuce! You never told me you had relations.
JANE. My uncle died and his wife cast me off.
ROCHESTER. Why?
JANE. I was poor and burdensome and she disliked me. *(A noticeable sniff from BLANCHE. ROCHESTER looks at BLANCHE disapprovingly and walks away with JANE.)*
ROCHESTER. You will come back; you must not be induced to stay for any reason.
JANE. I shall certainly return.

ROCHESTER. Well, you must have some money. How much do you have in the world? I have given you no salary yet.

JANE *(opening her purse).* Five shillings, sir.

ROCHESTER. Here, I have fifty pounds.

JANE. But you owe me but thirty—I have no change, sir.

ROCHESTER. Bring it back to me then.

JANE. I'd like to mention one other matter. You as good as informed me that you are going to be married.

ROCHESTER. Yes: what then?

JANE. In that case, sir, Adele ought to go to school.

ROCHESTER. To get her out of my bride's way you mean. And what about you?

JANE. I must seek another situation, somewhere.

ROCHESTER. You shall walk up the pyramids of Egypt! Give me back my fifty pounds!

JANE. But, I need it, sir.

ROCHESTER. Let me at least look at it.

JANE *(holding her purse behind her—they laugh).* No, sir: you are not to be trusted.

ROCHESTER. Jane! Promise me one thing.

JANE. I'll promise you anything that I am able to perform.

ROCHESTER. Do not advertise: if there is a post to be found, I will find it for you.

JANE. As long as you will promise that Adele and I will be safe out of the house before your bride enters it.

ROCHESTER. That I will promise. *(BLANCHE loudly bangs the piano, staring at him.)*

JANE *(extending her hand).* Farewell, sir.

ROCHESTER. Farewell then. *(He shakes her hand and moves away abruptly. The scene dissolves.)*

SCENE 15: GATESHEAD HALL

JANE. I returned to Gateshead.

(ADULT GEORGIANA and ELIZA appear. They are very formal.)

JANE. Miss Eliza. Miss Georgiana.
ELIZA. Miss Eyre.
GEORGIANA. How'd ya do.
JANE. I am very sorry for all your sad tidings. *(A sniff from GEORGIANA.)* I trust I am not too late. How is Mrs. Reed?
ELIZA. She sleeps now, but Death comes to us all.
JANE. What do you two plan to do?
ELIZA. We two? The day my mother's coffin is laid in Gateshead Church, I shall never more lay eyes on this fat, weak, puffy, selfish, useless thing known as my sister.
GEORGIANA. Selfish, ha! You should know!
ELIZA. I shall give my own fortune to a nunnery in France and spend the rest of my days there and never see her or this place again.
GEORGIANA. Yes, pray for your sins, you spiteful wretch! Much good may it do you. *(She bursts into tears.)*

(BESSIE enters.)

BESSIE *(embracing JANE).* Oh, Miss Jane. I knew you would come. Mrs. Reed is awake. Come with me.
JANE. I prepared to enter the red room, the room that had so terrified me when I was a child.

SCENE 16: THE RED ROOM

(MUSIC: Ominous and funereal. MRS. REED lies in her husband's bed—JANE approaches.)

MRS. REED. Is this Jane Eyre?

JANE. Yes, Aunt Reed. How are you, dear aunt? *(Touching her hand.)*

MRS. REED *(drawing her hand away)*. It is very warm tonight.

JANE. You sent for me, Aunt?

MRS. REED. Are you Jane Eyre?

JANE. I am Jane Eyre.

MRS. REED. I've had more trouble with that child than anyone would believe. Such an annoyance. She talked to me once like something mad. When the fever broke out at Lowood—I wished she had died.

JANE. Why do you hate her so?

MRS. REED. I hated my husband's sister for dying and leaving us with that child. He loved it. He made me promise to bring it up as my own—the crying, whining little brat. He made me promise!

JANE. Calm yourself, Aunt.

MRS. REED. Who calls me aunt?

JANE. I do. Jane Eyre.

MRS. REED. Oh, you ARE here. I have twice done you a wrong. One was to break the promise to my husband—the other—but why should I humble myself to you. Well—I must get it over. Eternity is before me. Go to my sewing case, open it and take out the letter you will see there. Read it. *(JANE removes the letter.)*

JANE. "Madam: Will you have the goodness to send me the address of my niece, Jane Eyre, and to tell me how she is: I desire her to come to see me in Madeira. As I am unmarried and childless, I wish to adopt my brother's child during my life and bequeath what I have to her upon my death. I am, Madam, John Eyre, Madeira." Why did I never hear of this?

MRS. REED. Because I disliked you so. The way you spoke to me.

JANE. Dear Mrs. Reed, forgive me for my passionate language, I was but a child then.

MRS. REED. I tell you I could not forget it and I took my revenge. I wrote him you were dead. "She died of typhoid at Lowood School." Do with this information what you will. I'm done with you and your bad disposition.

JANE. My disposition is not as bad as you think. I am passionate, but not vindictive. I should have been glad to love you, if you would have let me. Kiss me, now, dear aunt. *(JANE leans over to her. MRS. REED turns away.)*

MRS. REED. Too close. It oppresses me.

JANE. Love me; or hate me as you will. You have my full and free forgiveness: ask now for God's and be at peace.

(JANE moves away as MUSIC begins: the return to Thornfield.)

SCENE 17: THE RETURN and OUTSIDE THORNFIELD

JANE. I did not notify Mrs. Fairfax the exact day of my arrival: for I did not wish coach or carriage to meet me in Millcote. I longed to walk the old road through the fields to Thornfield. Why do I feel this joy as the road shortens before me? I know Mrs. Fairfax will smile me a calm welcome and dear Adele will clap her hands and throw her arms about me, but I know very well it is not them I think of, and I know very well that he is not thinking of me. Ah, but what a splendid midsummer evening! The hay has all been got in; the fields are green and shorn; sweet briar and southernwood, jasmine and rose yield their evening sacrifice of incense. *(She breathes deeply.)* And, ah, the great spreading chestnut tree... *(She looks out—sees it before her—curtsies.)* Hail! Noble guardian of Thornfield! *(She inhales deeply once more.)* But what is this new scent—Mr. Rochester's cigar!

(She attempts to retreat as light come up on ROCHESTER and the exterior of Thornfield. There is the great front door and a bench.)

ROCHESTER. And this is Jane Eyre? Coming on foot? Just like you to steal upon us at twilight like a ghost or a dream. What the deuce have you done with yourself this last month? Forgetting me quite, I'll be sworn.

JANE. I have been with my aunt, who is dead.

ROCHESTER. A true Janian reply! Come back from the dead like a fairy spirit to bewitch me—yes! Spirit, give me a charm to make me a handsome man! A handsome man for my new Mrs. Rochester.

JANE. That would be past the power of magic, sir.

ROCHESTER *(roaring with laughter)*. Leave it to you to tell it plain, Jane.

JANE. Then, you are going to be married, sir?

ROCHESTER. Ex-act-ly! Pre-cise-ly!

JANE. Soon, sir?

ROCHESTER. Very soon.

JANE. Then I must move on, sir?

ROCHESTER. Move on? Indeed you must.

JANE *(the blow hits her, she takes a moment to recover)*. Well—sir—I shall be ready when the order to march comes.

ROCHESTER. It is come now—I must give it tonight. *(JANE turns her head away—overcome.)* Jane! You're not turning your head away to look after moths, are you? I must remind you that it was you who said that in case I married, both you and little Adele would have to trot forthwith as my bride would not have it. So, Miss Eyre—you need a new situation?

JANE. Yes sir, I will advertise immediately.

ROCHESTER. Well, no need for that. I have an excellent post for you. The widow, Mrs. O'Gall, needs someone to educate her nine daughters—in Ireland.

JANE. Ireland? It is such a long way.

ROCHESTER. Across the sea, yes.

JANE. I shall be completely cut off—

ROCHESTER. Cut off?

JANE. From England—from Thornfield—from—

ROCHESTER. From?

JANE. From you, sir.

ROCHESTER. Ah, you'll forget me.

JANE. That I never should, sir.

ROCHESTER. Why, Jane? Are you sorry then to leave us?

JANE *(through her tears).* I grieve to leave Thornfield! I love Thornfield! I have lived in it a full and delightful life. I have not been trampled on. I have not been petrified. I have not been buried with inferior minds, but have talked face-to-face with a vigorous expanded mind. Yours, Mr. Rochester, I am so grateful to you for your great kindness and it strikes me with terror to feel I must be torn from you forever. It is like looking on the necessity of death.

ROCHESTER. Where do you see the necessity?

JANE. Where? In the shape of Miss Ingram; a noble and beautiful woman—your bride.

ROCHESTER. My bride!

JANE. Yes. And I must go, you have said it yourself.

ROCHESTER. No. I say you must stay!

JANE. I tell you I must go!

ROCHESTER. But, I want you to stay!

JANE *(passionately).* Do you think I can stay and become nothing to you? Do you think I am an automaton? A machine without feelings? Do you think because I am plain and poor, I am soulless and heartless? You think wrong! If God had gifted me with some beauty and much wealth, I should have made it as hard for you to leave me as it is now for me to leave you.

ROCHESTER. Jane... *(He puts his arms around her—she continues heatedly.)*

JANE. That you can wed one inferior to you—one I know you do not love and who does not truly love you. Let me go!

ROCHESTER. Where, Jane? To Ireland?

JANE. Yes—anywhere.

ROCHESTER *(restraining her)*. Jane, be still. Don't struggle so, my wild frantic bird...

JANE. I am no bird. No net ensnares me. I am a free human being with an independent will which I now use to leave you. *(JANE breaks free and hurries away. He stops her.)*

ROCHESTER. Then let your will decide your destiny. I offer you my hand; my heart; and a share of all I possess.

JANE. What farce is this?

ROCHESTER. I ask you to pass your life at my side—to be my second self.

JANE. For that fate you have already made your choice.

ROCHESTER. Yes! And that choice is you! My bride is here! Because my equal is here. Jane, will you marry me? *(No answer.)* Do you doubt me, Jane?

JANE. Entirely.

ROCHESTER. You have no faith in me?

JANE. Not a whit!

ROCHESTER. Am I a liar then? Here is the truth—you are right—I do not love Miss Ingram and indeed she does not love me. In fact, I started a rumor that I was worth less than a third of what she supposed and she and her mother promptly gave me the cold shoulder. But, I could not marry Miss Ingram in any case. I love you as my own flesh.

JANE. Me?

ROCHESTER. You, Jane. I must have you for my own—say yes, quickly! *(She is dumbstruck.)* Oh, Jane, you torture me!

JANE. Your feelings are true—your offer is real?

ROCHESTER. Say—"Edward—I will marry you."

JANE. You truly love me?
ROCHESTER. I do.
JANE. Then, sir, I will marry you.
ROCHESTER. "Edward"—my little wife!
JANE. My dear Edward!
ROCHESTER *(embracing her).* God pardon me! I have you and will hold you. Make my happiness and I will make yours. Are you happy, Jane?
JANE. Yes. *(MUSIC as thunder—rain begins.)*
ROCHESTER. We must go in! Though I could stay till morning here with you.
JANE. And so could I with you! *(They kiss fervently as the rain pours down. There is a sudden blinding flash of lightning and a thunderclap. The both look out amazed. The sound of a great tree falling is heard.)* The chestnut tree! Oh, Edward—it has been split in two!

(Another great thunderclap as MRS. FAIRFAX opens the door of Thornfield and sees ROCHESTER holding JANE in his arms. They realize she is there and quickly enter the house as MRS. FAIRFAX slowly closes the door—a deeply troubled look on her face. Over the wind and thunder, a wild laugh is heard.)

END OF ACT ONE

ACT TWO

SCENE 1: JANE'S BEDROOM AND THE ENTRANCE HALL

AT RISE: *MUSIC: Again, the romantic, melancholy theme. The wedding dress is laid out. JANE is being dressed for her wedding by LEAH. ADELE, charmingly attired, examines the wedding bouquet. Below, JOHN is hauling trunks outside under the supervision of ROCHESTER. MRS. FAIRFAX passes them making her way to JANE's room with a tea tray.)*

JANE. You are sure you checked the post, Leah?
LEAH. Yes, ma'am. No letter has come.
ROCHESTER. John, how many trunks are left?
JOHN. Three, sir.
ROCHESTER. Good. I want all in readiness for our departure the minute the ceremony is complete. *(Intercepting MRS. FAIRFAX.)* Whose tea is that?
MRS. FAIRFAX. Miss Eyre's, sir.
ROCHESTER. Give me that. In thirty minutes it will be, Mrs. Rochester's. *(He grabs the tray and bounds up the stairs.)*
MRS. FAIRFAX. Really, sir. She is dressing.
ROCHESTER. Knock. Knock. Tea service.
JANE. Mr. Rochester!
ROCHESTER. Edward! Knock! Knock!

JANE. Adele! *Allez a la porte!*

ADELE. *Non, non, monsieur! N'entrez pas!*

ROCHESTER. Tell the future Mrs. Rochester, I would have a word with her. *Ouvrez la porte!*

MRS. FAIRFAX *(taking the tea and squeezing by him).* Really, sir, you will spill the tea on your fine suit.

JANE *(coming to the door).* What do you want, sir.

ROCHESTER. I want to see you.

JANE. That you cannot.

ROCHESTER. I want to marry you.

JANE. That you can—if you will let me complete my toilette, sir.

ROCHESTER. Have you put on the pearl necklace I gave you?

JANE. Yes, sir.

ROCHESTER. The veil?

JANE. Not yet, sir.

ROCHESTER. I wish you would have let me put a diamond circlet in your hair and sparkling bracelets on your fine wrists, my beauty.

JANE. Don't address me as such; I am still your plain Jane.

ROCHESTER. You are a beauty in my eyes. You will wear what I have bought you for the honeymoon?

JANE. Yes! Yes, once you have married me, yes. Talk to him, Adele. In English.

ADELE. Where are you taking *mademoiselle*?

ROCHESTER. To the moon.

ADELE. She will be cold.

ROCHESTER. Fire rises out of the lunar mountains.

ADELE. She will be lonely with only you on the moon.

ROCHESTER. Then we will send for you to visit us.

ADELE. There is no road to the moon.

ROCHESTER *(picking her up and running her down the stairs)*. We will fly! *(She laughs merrily.)* John, is everything packed?

JOHN. Yes, sir. Everything. The horses are being harnessed.

ROCHESTER. Is the clergyman come yet.

JOHN. No, sir.

ROCHESTER. He daren't be late. *(He rushes off to have a look.)*

MRS. FAIRFAX. Drink something, Miss Eyre. You will faint.

JANE. I'm too excited. Mrs. Fairfax—there was no letter come for me.

MRS. FAIRFAX. None, dear.

JANE. Oh, I wanted so to hear from my uncle. To suddenly realize you have a relation—to let him know I'm to be married. I hope he received my letter.

MRS. FAIRFAX. I will forward any news to you on your honeymoon. Now, Leah, the veil? *(LEAH opens the armoire and brings out a very long veil which has been ripped to pieces.)*

LEAH. Oh no! Oh, Miss Eyre, oh no! *(They all rush to the veil.)*

MRS. FAIRFAX. It has been torn to shreds! Look at this! Who would do this?

JANE *(holding it before her)*. It must have happened in the night while I slept. I dreamed of such a thing. I suppose it wasn't a dream.

ROCHESTER *(calling from below)*. The clergyman is arriving. Is my future wife ready?

MRS. FAIRFAX *(calling down)*. Yes, sir. A moment. *(Back to JANE.)* What is to be done? Mr. Rochester bought this for you. Dear Lord!

JANE *(pulling a box from the bottom of the armoire)*. Pin this on, Leah. It is what I intended before giving in to his finery.

(They attach a small plain square of blond as MR. WOOD, the clergyman arrives below.)

ROCHESTER. Come in, sir. If you will wait here, I will fetch the bride. *(He bounds up the stairs.)* Jane! Lingerer, my brain is on fire with impatience, you tarry so long!

(He raps at door. ADELE opens it. He admires JANE.)

ROCHESTER. Fair as a lily—but what is this? Even now, you exercise your will and shun my gift.
JANE. No, sir. No. The veil has been rent. I cannot wear it. It happened in the night.
ROCHESTER. While you slept? *(She nods. He clutches her to him.)* Thank God! Only the veil was harmed—to think what might have happened! We must not delay an instant. Come. Everyone to your place! We're ready to start!

(He takes her by the hand—leads her down the stairs. All follow and gather around MR. WOOD in his surplice, holding a prayer book.)

ROCHESTER. You may begin, sir.
MR. WOOD. We are gathered here to witness the holy bond of matrimony between Mr. Edward Fairfax Rochester and Miss Jane Eyre.

(GRACE POOLE is seen standing outside her door. A STRANGER enters and approaches the wedding party.)

MR. WOOD. I require and charge you both, that if either of you or any present know of any impediment why ye may not be lawfully joined together in matrimony; now confess it.

THE STRANGER (BRIGGS). The marriage cannot go on: I declare the existence of an impediment. *(All look to the speaker except ROCHESTER.)*

ROCHESTER *(to MR. WOOD)*. Proceed.

MR. WOOD. I cannot proceed without some investigation into what has been asserted. Sir?

MR. BRIGGS *(coming forward)*. There exists a previous marriage. Mr. Rochester has a wife now living. *(A profound pause. ROCHESTER slowly turns.)*

ROCHESTER. Who are you?

BRIGGS. My name is Briggs, sir, solicitor for Mr. Richard Mason.

ROCHESTER. You would thrust on me a wife?

BRIGGS. I would remind you, sir, of the lady's existence; which the law recognizes if you do not. You married her fifteen years ago and she was living still three months ago. I have a witness to the fact.

ROCHESTER. Produce him—or go to hell.

BRIGGS. Mr. Mason—have the goodness to step forward.

(RICHARD MASON appears and timidly comes forward.)

ROCHESTER. Well, Mason, what have you to say? *(No answer.)* What have you to say?

MASON. Edward Rochester married my sister, Bertha Antoinetta Mason, fifteen years ago in Spanish Town, Jamaica. I have a copy of the record found in the register. Last April, I saw her in Thornfield Hall.

MR. WOOD. Impossible! I am an old resident of this neighborhood, sir, and I never heard of a Mrs. Rochester.

ROCHESTER *(almost a snarl).* No, by God! I took care that none should hear of it. Enough! Wood, close your book, and take off your surplice! There will be no wedding today. Bigamy is an ugly word! I meant, however, to be a bigamist: but fate has out-maneuvered me. What this lawyer and his client say is true: I have been married. And the woman lives! Yes, Bertha Mason lives. And Bertha Mason is mad! My father married me off for money into a family of lunatics. Her mother, who I was told was dead, was in an asylum. Her younger brother in the mad-house as well. You, Dick, are probably soon to follow. Do you want to see what sort of being I was cheated into marrying? I invite you all to come upstairs and visit Mrs. Poole's patient—my wife!

(He drags JANE and leads them all up the stairs.)

ROCHESTER. Unhitch the horse, John. No bride leaves here today. You know the place we go to, Mason—she bit and stabbed you here. *(At the door to GRACE POOLE's room.)* This young girl knows nothing of the wretch you are about to see. She thought all was fair and legal and never dreamt she was going to be entrapped into a feigned union with a partner already wedded to this! *(He flings open the door. The inner room is revealed for the first time.)*

SCENE 2: BERTHA'S ROOM

(GRACE POOLE stands by the door. Against the opposite wall crouches BERTHA MASON, growling like a caged animal, in a muslin gown with a wild mane of dark hair.)

ROCHESTER. How is your charge today, Mrs. Poole?
GRACE POOLE. Take care, sir. She sees you! For God's sake, take care! She's clever. *(BERTHA lets out a frightening animal scream. She pulls back her hair and gazes wildly at the visitors.)*
ROCHESTER. Keep out of the way. *(BERTHA springs at ROCHESTER. She jumps on him, clawing wildly at his face, attempting to bite him. A terrifying struggle ensues between the two. At one point, BERTHA breaks from ROCHESTER and runs at JANE. It is now that he catches her from behind and forces her into a chair. She screams wildly.)* Bind her, Grace. *(GRACE ties her securely to the chair.)* There sits my wife. You've seen the sole conjugal embrace I am able to know. You've heard the endearments which are my solace! And there stands what I wished to have. This young girl, so grave and quiet at the mouth of hell. Compare these clear eyes with these red balls of fire—this sweet face—with this monstrous mask—this tender mercy—with this rough revenge: then judge me, and remember, with what judgment ye judge shall ye be judged. Off with all of you! I must shut up my prize! *(They all withdraw. Leaving ROCHESTER with GRACE and BERTHA as the room recedes. All precede JANE, BRIGGS and MASON down the stairs.)*

SCENE 3: THE HALL AND JANE'S BEDROOM

MR. BRIGGS *(to JANE)*. You, madam, are cleared of all blame: your uncle will be glad to hear of it.

JANE. My uncle?

MASON. I was staying with Mr. Eyre in Madeira on my way back to Jamaica, when he received your letter announcing your marriage to Rochester. I informed him of the grim reality, and being too ill to travel himself, he asked me to return to help extricate you from this marriage. I am thankful we were not too late, as doubtless you are also.

BRIGGS. As I am certain that Mr. Eyre will be dead before you could reach Madeira, I'd advise you to remain in England until we hear further word of Mr. Eyre. Can we assist you further?

JANE. No, no.

BRIGGS. Good day then. *(They both bow and go.)*

(MUSIC. JANE, now alone, goes into her room and bolts the door. In a trance, she removes her wedding dress, veil, necklace, and puts on her old dress. She lays everything out neatly on the bed. After a time, a disheveled ROCHESTER comes to her door and sinks onto the floor waiting for her to come out.)

JANE. A Christmas frost has come at midsummer; a white December storm has whirled over June; ice has glazed the ripe apples, drifts crushed the blushing roses; my hopes are dead. Struck down as in one night befell all the first-born of Egypt. My cherished wishes of yesterday as livid corpses today. Oh, how blind my eyes! How weak my conduct! Never more to turn to him. Never more to seek his arms. What am I to do? I must leave Thornfield at once.

(She opens her door and nearly trips over ROCHESTER.)

ROCHESTER. Jane, Jane—I was wrong ever to bring you to Thornfield. I charged them all to conceal from you the fiend that lay within this stone hell; I did this at first because I feared Adele would never have a governess to stay if she knew what inmate was housed here, but then, when it was you, I feared for my very life that you would leave me. I tested you in every way. I made you jealous of foolish Blanche, who I never loved. I love you. Only you. From the first night when you overthrew me and my horse, I was forever overthrown. Jane, I'll close up Thornfield and give Mrs. Poole two hundred a year to live here with her. I have a property in the south of France: a white-washed villa on the shores of the Mediterranean. There no one will know us. You WILL be my wife there. We can live happy—Jane, don't shake your head. You don't love me, Jane?

JANE. I do love you, but this is the last time I must express it. Your wife is living, sir, if I were to live with you as you desire, I would then be your mistress: to say otherwise is false.

ROCHESTER. Jane, for the first time in my life I have found what I can truly love—I have found you. Jane, give me your promise—say "I will be yours, Mr. Rochester."

JANE. Mr. Rochester, I will NOT be yours.

ROCHESTER. Do you mean to abandon me, then?

JANE. I do.

ROCHESTER. Jane, do you mean it now? *(He bends and kisses her on her brow.)*

JANE. No, don't, sir.

ROCHESTER. Oh, you can't be kissed by the husband of Bertha Mason! Shall I give all my kisses to her? Jane! What in God's name am I to do?

JANE. Do as I do: trust in God.

ROCHESTER. God? No, you fling me back to a life of dissipation and vice.

JANE. I no more assign this fate to you than I grasp it for myself.

ROCHESTER. Jane, you have no relatives whom you fear to offend by living with me! No one will care.

JANE. I care! I care for myself! I have a worth to myself, so I have always believed and if I can't believe it now then I am insane—quite insane. *(Both are silent for a long moment.)*

ROCHESTER *(quiet, resigned)*. You would leave me, then?

JANE. Yes. *(ROCHESTER, with a tremendous sob, struggles to the door. He fumbles to open it. JANE goes to him, laying her head on his back.)*

ROCHESTER. Oh, Jane! I never meant to hurt you thus!

JANE. I know.

ROCHESTER. My love. My life.

JANE God bless you and keep you from harm and reward you for all your past kindness to me.

ROCHESTER. Your love would have been my reward. Oh, Jane, think on it. Think on it now. Let your heart change or mine is broken.

(He leaves her and staggers down the hall and out of sight. JANE immediately picks up her hat, her bag and runs from Thornfield. A tight light on JANE's tear-streaked face as the stage clears to an empty void.)

JANE. I ran. Ran from Thornfield. Ran from every happiness I had known. Ran. A mile from the Hall a coach stopped, I said "How far do you go?" He named a place a long way off, where I knew Mr. Rochester had no connections. I gave the driver all I had—twenty shillings—and said "Take me there." *(The sound of a speeding coach becomes deafening as the lights black out.)*

SCENE 4: JANE'S JOURNEY

(MUSIC: Driving like the storm—thunder—rain. Lights up on JANE wandering desolate, her hair streaming, her belongings gone. She wanders helplessly—stops a PEASANT.)

JANE. Please, do you know of a place in the neighborhood that needs a servant?
PEASANT WOMAN. No place that I know of.
JANE. What do most people do here?
WOMAN. They are farm labourers or work in Mr. Oliver's needle factory.
JANE. Does he employ women?
WOMAN. Nay: it's men's work.
JANE. What is a woman to do?
WOMAN. Get on as best she can.

(The WOMAN hurries away. JANE moves on. A church bell tolls. An OLD LADY opens a parsonage door.)

JANE. Is the clergyman at home?
OLD LADY. No.
JANE. Will he return soon?
OLD LADY. No. He's gone far from home.
JANE. Please, I haven't eaten anything for three days. Could you give me a roll or a crust of bread for this handkerchief?
OLD LADY. How do I know where you got it?
JANE. Please, take it.
OLD LADY. No! *(She slams the door. It gets darker. Sound of doors slamming, one after another. Guard dogs barking.)*
JANE. Oh, Providence! Sustain me a little longer. Aid—direct me.

(She walks on and on. Slowly, out of the distance, a cottage moves toward her. A cheery light in the window. Collapsing, she knocks on the door. The servant, HANNAH, an old country woman, opens the door holding a candle.)

SCENE 5: MARSH END

HANNAH. What do you want?
JANE. Please, a night's shelter in some outbuilding and a morsel of bread.
HANNAH. We can't take in a vagrant to lodge.
JANE. Where shall I go if you drive me away?

HANNAH. Oh, I warrant you know where to go well enough.

JANE. I have no strength to go—Don't shut the door, oh, for God's sake. *(HANNAH attempts to shut the door. JANE slides weakly to the ground.)* I must die, then.

(ST. JOHN RIVERS enters—a tall, very handsome and intense man.)

ST. JOHN. All men must die, but are not condemned to meet a premature doom, as yours would be if you perished here?

HANNAH. Is it you, Mr. St. John?

ST. JOHN. Yes—yes, open quickly. You have done your duty in excluding, now let me do mine in admitting. Come with me.

(He helps JANE into the house. Darkness. The storm peaks and subsides. It is now four days later. HANNAH is at work in the kitchen. DIANA and MARY RIVERS, two young women, are at work repairing JANE's cloak in the parlor. ST. JOHN reads his Bible.)

DIANA. Thank God, brother, you brought that poor stranger in.

MARY. She would certainly have been found dead on our doorstep. I wonder what she has suffered?

DIANA. Strange hardships, I am sure, though she has spoken not a word.

MARY. Her clothes were fine enough, they require very little mending for all she must have been through.

(JANE, now up and dressed, enters the kitchen opposite and startles HANNAH.)

HANNAH. What, you have got up? Come, sit you down.

JANE *(weakly takes a seat)*. How long was I sleeping?

HANNAH. Four days now. Did you ever go a-begging before?

JANE *(bristling)*. I am no beggar: any more than yourself.

HANNAH. I don't understand that? You've no house or no brass, have you?

JANE. The want of house or brass, by which I take it you mean money, does not a beggar make. If you are a Christian, you ought not to think poverty a crime. You turned me out on a night when you would not have shut out a dog.

HANNAH. I was wrong to do such, miss. Mr. St. John tells me so, too. I was thinking of the young ladies, not myself, but I'm begging of you now, your forgiveness.

JANE. That you have—shake hands. *(They do.)* Are those gooseberries?

HANNAH. For the pies, yes.

JANE. Let me help you.

(She begins preparing the berries as DIANA and MARY cross into the room.)

MARY. Miss!

DIANA. Oh, you should not have gotten up without my leave. *(She feels JANE's forehead.)* The fever is gone.

JANE. I am very well here. Please tell me your names.

MARY. I am Mary Rivers, this is my sister, Diana. *(Calling to ST. JOHN.)* Brother, she is up!

JANE. You live here with Mr. St. John?

DIANA. No, none of us. This was our father's house. He died three weeks ago and we all came here to be with him till the end. Mary and I will soon return to Manchester where we are governesses and our brother will return to his parish.

JANE. He is a parson?

(ST. JOHN crosses in behind his sisters.)

ST. JOHN. I am a parson, yes, in Morton. And what is your name?

JANE. It's Jane—Jane—Elliot. That name is the one I think best to use at present, though it is not my own.

ST. JOHN. Your real name you will not give?

JANE. I fear discovery above all things and must do all I can to avoid it.

DIANA. Can we send to anyone on your behalf?

JANE. No one. No. I have no home now. Do not think I am ungrateful, but I protect my own security and that of others.

ST. JOHN. What do you propose to do now?

JANE. Sir, I beg of your generosity, one more favor. Help me to find work. I am a teacher, but will do any honest labour I can.

DIANA. Brother, this is providential.

MARY. Perhaps, both your searches can end here.

ST. JOHN. Miss Elliot, as you call yourself, it happens that I may have a position. Meager, obscure, but honest. When I came to Morton two years ago, they had no school. I was able to start one for boys and now I mean to open one for girls—what is wanted is the teacher. The girls are poor, uneducated—the school is but one room—the pay thirty pound a year and you will not be able to utilize even a fraction of your mental powers—

JANE. Sir, sir—say no more. I accept your kind offer, with all my heart.

(MUSIC: Awkward singing of the hymn "Walk With Me." Roughly, but cleanly dressed SCHOOLGIRLS begin to enter and assemble in a simple classroom. JANE will take her place there as teacher momentarily. HANNAH and ST. JOHN exit. MARY and DIANA are left to bid farewell to JANE.)

DIANA. An angel has looked down on us by bringing you here. Jane, you will be a tremendous help to our brother and perhaps, in time, can dissuade him from his course.

JANE. What course?

MARY. Now that Father is gone, our brother intends to take upon himself the missionary life. He will probably go to India and, although we know it is right, noble and Christian, it breaks our hearts.

DIANA. We may soon have to sell this, our family home, for it is all that is left to us. Then we will be without home or brother, two governesses alone in the world. Surely, you can understand our feelings.

MARY. If only he could find strength and satisfaction in his calling here.

DIANA. But I tell you he is inexorable as death.

MARY. Perhaps, you might help him to see this.

JANE. If I can, dear ones, I will.

DIANA and MARY. Thank you, dear Jane, and farewell. *(They go.)*

SCENE 6: MORTON SCHOOL

JANE. My first days at Morton School were humbling. Only three of the girls could read at all. My lessons were of the most basic studies. No French or geography here, but then, those subjects would only have reminded me that had I made a different choice I might now be living in France, with the man I loved—in a fool's paradise. Here—a paradise of fools. But as the weeks proceeded, my girls applied themselves and I saw definite progress. The school was established by Mr. Oliver, the owner of the needle factory. His daughter, Rosamund, saw to my needs and would often visit just as Mr. St. John was giving his catechism lesson.

(JANE turns to the class as ST. JOHN finishes.)

JANE. Young ladies, this concludes your morning lessons. Thank Mr. Rivers—
GIRLS. Thank you, Mr. Rivers.
JANE. Ah, and here is our benefactress. Please say good day to Miss Oliver as you go out.

(The GIRLS file past the beautiful young woman who has just entered in a handsome riding habit—ROSAMUND OLIVER.)

ROSAMUND. Good morning, all, Miss Elliot, Mr. St. John. I rode up with your mail to save you the trip into town.
ST. JOHN. Thank you. *(He takes the mail and looks through it, avoiding ROSAMUND.)*

ROSAMUND. Miss Jane, I trust all continues well with your scholars.

JANE. Very well.

ROSAMUND. I should like to come up and help you teach. It will be a change for me now and then.

JANE. The girls would enjoy that greatly.

ROSAMUND. Mr. Rivers, Father has asked why you have not been to visit him? He is alone this evening, would you like to return with me?

ST. JOHN. Not tonight, Miss Rosamund.

ROSAMUND. Oh, but he would very much enjoy your visit and I know how sad you must be now with your sisters returned to Manchester and Marsh End closed up.

ST. JOHN. Thank you, but this evening I must reply urgently to this letter.

ROSAMUND. Nothing serious, I trust?

ST. JOHN. It seems my uncle John has died—

JANE. Oh, Mr. Rivers—

ST. JOHN. We did not know each other very well. There had been a rift within our family. In any case, he has left his entire estate to a relative that cannot be found, otherwise, my sisters and I would be the heirs.

ROSAMUND. Oh, dear!

ST. JOHN. At any rate, I must reply. Please excuse me—

ROSAMUND *(catches his arm as he goes)*. Promise me you will come tomorrow evening.

ST. JOHN *(quietly, without looking directly at her)*. I will come. *(He goes.)*

ROSAMUND *(coming to JANE's desk)*. Ah, he is one of God's angels.

JANE. He is indeed.

Act II   JANE EYRE   91

ROSAMUND. Father feels so too. He says it is a pity that such a fine young man should want to go off to India, a missionary, when he could have quite a valuable life here.

JANE. You, I take it, are of the same opinion.

ROSAMUND. Oh yes, very much so. Miss Jane, what are these drawings?

JANE. They are mine.

ROSAMUND. These are very fine indeed. Miss Jane, would you sketch my portrait? Papa would so love a portrait.

JANE. I would be honored. *(ROSAMUND sits and poses as JANE addresses AUDIENCE.)* I felt a thrill of artist's delight at the idea of copying so perfect and radiant a model. I sketched a fine likeness. *(She shows portrait to ROSAMUND who smiles delightedly, then exits.)* It gave me great pleasure to draw Mr. Rivers' unrequited love. I felt strangely closer to him in our mutual loneliness. If only I could help him to act upon the wishes of his heart.

(ST. JOHN is now in the room.)

JANE. Mr. Rivers! Tell me, is this portrait like?

ST. JOHN. Like whom?

JANE. Surely you recognize her.

ST. JOHN. Oh, yes. Miss Rosamund, I presume. A well-executed picture, very graceful, very correct.

JANE. As a reward for your accurate guess, I will promise to paint you a faithful duplicate, if that would be acceptable to you.

ST. JOHN *(still gazing at the picture).* It is very like; the expression is perfect—it smiles.

JANE. When you are in India, would it comfort or pain you to have this painting?

ST. JOHN. That I should like to have it is certain, but is it wise? I am not certain.

JANE. Wouldn't it be wiser to take to yourself the original, she likes you I am sure of it and her father respects you as well.

ST. JOHN. DOES she like me?

JANE. Better than anyone else, I am sure of it.

ST. JOHN. It is strange that while I love Rosamund so wildly—I experience at the same time the calm knowledge she would not make me a good wife.

JANE. Why?

ST. JOHN. She is not the partner suited to me. Rosamund a sufferer? A labourer? A missionary's wife? Never!

JANE. But you might relinquish that vocation.

ST. JOHN. Relinquish! My great work? My foundation laid on earth for my mansion in heaven? It is dearer than the blood in my veins—all that I live for.

JANE. But what of Miss Oliver's feelings?

ST. JOHN. She is ever surrounded by suitors and flatterers. Some other will claim her affection in time.

JANE. You tremble whenever you see her!

ST. JOHN. She is well named—the Rose of the World. But, it is a weakness on my part that I scorn. A mere fever of the flesh and I will be as firm and fixed as a rock.

JANE. Would you like the painting then?

ST. JOHN. No. *(He takes one last look and goes to hand back the picture. Suddenly his eye is caught by some-*

thing on the paper. He rips off a piece, stuffs it in his pocket, then hands it back.) Good afternoon.

JANE. His sister was correct—he is inexorable as death. *(It begins to snow.)* The weeks went on. St. John avoided Rosamund by burying himself in his studies and visiting the sick and needy. I had not seen either of them due to the snow.

ST. JOHN. I must have a little talk with you.

JANE. Yes?

ST. JOHN. I have a story to relate that you will find quite fantastic. Do you remember the letter I received telling me of my uncle's death and the missing heir.

JANE. Yes.

ST. JOHN. The heir has been found, I believe.

JANE. Yes?

ST. JOHN. Yes. My mother had two brothers. One married a rich man's daughter but they both died leaving an orphaned girl. She was sent off to live with her mother's brother. But he promptly died, so the orphan was reared by his wife—a Mrs. Reed of Gateshead. You start! Did you hear a noise? Well, my mother's other brother engaged my father in a business deal which left him penniless. My father never forgave him. But, this uncle went on to make his fortune and because of his rift with our family, left all he had to this orphaned girl. His name is John Eyre of Madeira, my mother's maiden name is Eyre. The name of the orphaned heir is Jane Eyre.

JANE. Mr. Rivers!

ST. JOHN. A Mr. Briggs wrote to me of this and I knew nothing until the other day when I looked at Jane Elliot's sketch pad and saw traced in India ink on the margin the name—Jane Eyre. Could you shed some light on this for me?

JANE. You already know so much, it is now for you to tell me.

ST. JOHN. I merely tell you that John Eyre of Madeira has left you all his property and that you are now rich—nothing more.

JANE. I? Rich?

ST. JOHN. You must prove your identity, of course, but that should pose no problem. Don't you want to know how much you are worth?

JANE *(pacing back and forth)*. How much am I worth?

ST. JOHN. A trifle—twenty thousand pounds.

JANE. Twenty?

ST. JOHN. Well, if you had committed murder you could scarcely look more aghast.

JANE. Perhaps you read the figures wrong—it may be two thousand.

ST. JOHN. It is written in letters—twenty thousand. So—now I must leave you to your sorrows. Good night.

JANE. Stop one minute!

ST. JOHN. Well?

JANE. Your mother was my father's sister?

ST. JOHN. Yes.

JANE. My uncle John was your uncle John?

ST. JOHN. Undeniably.

JANE. You three—Diana, Mary and yourself, then—are my cousins?

ST. JOHN. We are cousins; yes.

JANE. Oh! I am glad! I am so glad! I had nobody; and now I have three relations! In one moment three relations!

ST. JOHN. In one moment—twenty thousand pounds.

JANE. We are four? Twenty thousand pounds shared equally will be five thousand pounds each! Write to Diana tomorrow and tell them to come home directly!

ST. JOHN. You must really make an effort to tranquilize your feelings.

JANE. Have you no excitement over our good fortune?

ST. JOHN. YOUR good fortune. The money was left solely to you. It is your right.

JANE. And I say five thousand is more than enough for me, twenty thousand would torment and oppress me. I am resolved that you three, who have given me back my life, will share in this with me. I have never had a home, I never had brother or sisters; I must and will have them now.

ST. JOHN. You have us without sacrificing your rights.

JANE. Sacrifice? I who had thirty pounds a year, now have five thousand! I see no sacrifice! OH, St. John, I want to open up Marsh End and live there in our family home. You won't have to sell it now and the four of us will be together there at Christmas! No more arguments! We will celebrate the best Christmas we have ever had!

SCENE 7: MARSH END

(MUSIC. Marsh End reappears now transformed with new curtains and fine furnishings. Everything sparkles and glows with holiday cheer. HANNAH is taking fresh pies from the oven. DIANA and MARY come running in to embrace JANE. ST. JOHN stands apart.)

DIANA and MARY. Jane! Sister! *(Laughing and hugging.)*

JANE. Diana, Mary! Oh, my dears, this is a happy day. *(DIANA and MARY run to HANNAH and embrace her. JANE turns to ST. JOHN.)* And where is your happiness? Why such a troubled brow?

ST. JOHN. Jane, I hope you will not continue to put all your energies into commonplace home pleasures.

JANE. St. John, you are most wicked to talk so. I am disposed to be as content as a queen.

ST. JOHN. God meant for you to do more than this, do you hear me, Jane?

JANE. I hear you just as if you were speaking Greek. I have adequate cause to be happy and I WILL be happy!

(DIANA and MARY return.)

DIANA. Brother! What effect has our bequest had upon you? Will it keep you in England and married to Rosamund Oliver?

ST. JOHN. Rosamund Oliver is to be married to Mr. Granby, heir to Sir Frederick Granby.

MARY. St. John! They could not have known each other long.

ST. JOHN. Things happen quickly when there are no obstacles in their way. And as I plan to leave for India at winter's end, it is just as well. In fact, now that you are all here, you could be a help to me in my preparation. Jane, would you study Hindostanee with me, so that I may hasten my familiarity with the language.

JANE. If you want, sir.

DIANA. He'd never have persuaded me to it, Jane. Hindostanee! But, why speak of this now? Come, brother, you have not even given your sisters a kiss!

ST. JOHN. Yes, Diana, you are right. *(He kisses her.)* Mary. *(He kisses her.)*

DIANA. You forget, you have a third sister now. You may kiss her too.

(She pushes JANE toward him. Awkwardly, they kiss. Then JANE comes forward to the AUDIENCE, as the girls join HANNAH in the kitchen and ST. JOHN resumes studying in the parlour.)

JANE. There are no such things as marble kisses or ice kisses, or I should say St. John's kiss was surely one of these. I knew the difference. His kiss heated me only because of the memory of someone else's kisses. Now that I was independent, I had to know of Mr. Rochester. I wrote to Mrs. Fairfax, but received no reply. Perhaps something had happened to my first letter. I wrote again and while waiting for the answer, continued in my studies.

ST. JOHN. Jane, I go in six weeks.

JANE. God will protect you, for you have undertaken his work.

ST. JOHN. Jane, come with me to India: be my help-mate and fellow labourer.

JANE. Oh, St. John, have some mercy!

ST. JOHN. God has intended you for a missionary's wife. And a missionary's wife you must be.

JANE. Wife?

ST. JOHN. I claim you—not for my pleasure, but for God's service.

JANE. I am not fit for such service.

ST. JOHN. Who ever is? Humility, Jane, becomes you. I have observed you, Jane. Tested you ever since I've known you. Your work with the girls at Morton School. The diligence with which you undertake every task and challenge presented to you. You could conduct the Indian schools and help the Indian women.

JANE. But you ask me to go as your wife?

ST. JOHN. It must be so. We will constantly be together in solitudes—in savage crowds—you must give your heart to God.

JANE. I may be able to give my heart to God—but not to you. You do not want it. You are my comrade, my adopted brother, but my lover you are not. I scorn your idea of love.

ST. JOHN. I think I have uttered nothing to deserve scorn.

JANE. Forgive my words, St. John: but you have raised a topic on which our natures are at variance: the very name of love strikes a discord between us. My dear cousin, abandon your scheme of marriage.

ST. JOHN. We could learn to love each other in time. But, in my opinion, you are not formed for love, but for labour.

JANE. If I am not formed for love, then it follows that I am not formed for marriage. Should I be chained for life to someone who regards me as a useful tool? *(She begins to laugh.)* To think that once I scorned the love of a man who loved me body and soul because his love was not legitimate. And now—with a legitimate marriage proposal before me—I am asked to marry for no love at all.

ST. JOHN. Jane, you must put these sinful thoughts from your mind. Kneel, Jane and pray with me. Kneel. *(They do.)* Remember, your Scripture, Jane. Revelation: Chapter twenty-one. "And I saw a new heaven and a new earth. He that overcometh shall inherit all things. But, the fearful and unbelieving, and the abominable, and murderers, and whoremongers, and sorcerers and idolaters, and all liars..."

(As he speaks, the lights have come down to just a special on JANE's face. A lighting effect of burning fire begins to surround them as other voices are heard and we see PEOPLE emerging from the shadows.)

JOHN REED. She's a liar! A liar!

ST. JOHN. "...shall have their part in the lake that burneth with fire and brimstone: which is the second death."

BROCKLEHURST. Do you know where the wicked go after death? They go to hell. A pit full of fire! A pit full of fire! Should you like to fall into the pit and be burning there forever?

ST. JOHN *(simultaneously with BROCKLEHURST)*. Jane! "All shall have their part in the lake that burneth with fire and brimstone: fire and brimstone, fire and brimstone, fire and brimstone..."

YOUNG JANE. You think that I can do without one bit of love, but I cannot live so.

ST. JOHN. "...which is the second death!"

MRS. REED. I wrote him you were dead.

HELEN. Besides this earth, there is an invisible world and a kingdom of spirits; those spirits watch us and they guard us, Jane.

ROCHESTER'S VOICE. Jane! Jane! Jane!

ST. JOHN. "A lake that burneth with fire!"

(A vision appears of BERTHA—high in the air as though on ramparts—the wind blows her hair and gown—she stands with her arms raised—screaming.)

JANE. Oh, God, what is it?

ST. JOHN. What have you heard, Jane? Do you hear the voice crying in the wilderness, Jane? Lay your hand upon the Christian cross and the angel's crown! Jane! *(He embraces her with religious fervor.)*

ROCHESTER'S VOICE. Jane! Jane! Jane!

JANE. I am coming! Wait for me! *(She breaks free of ST. JOHN. Everything disappears.)*

ST. JOHN. Jane?

JANE. Oh, I will come.

ST. JOHN. Jane!

JANE. Ask me no more questions—make no more remarks! Leave me: I must and will be alone.

ST. JOHN. Jane!

JANE. I must and will be alone!

SCENE 8: THE RUINS OF THORNFIELD

(MRS. FAIRFAX is coming upon JANE. We are now back at the ruins of Thornfield Hall. All else is gone.)

FAIRFAX. Jane! Is it really you, Jane—Jane Eyre—come to this lonely place?

JANE. Mrs. Fairfax! *(She rushes to embrace her.)* Oh, Mrs. Fairfax, what has happened to Thornfield Hall?

MRS. FAIRFAX. It burnt down at harvest time; dreadful. Hardly any of the furniture could be saved. It broke out in the dead of night, before the engines could arrive the house was one mass of flame.

JANE. How did it originate?

MRS. FAIRFAX. I think you can guess. Grace Poole would drink and when she fell off to sleep, Mrs. Rochester got free. She must have gone directly to your room, for the fire started there. The house was aroused. She was running wild from place to place. Mr. Rochester went to the attics and got the servants out of their beds. I got Adele out. That's when I saw her. She was on the roof. She stood there waving her arms and screaming on the battlements. Mr. Rochester called to her and then tried to approach. Flames were darting up all about them. Just as he got to her, she let forth a wild laugh and leapt off—her white gown and hair streaming about her as she fell to the pavement.

JANE. Dead?

MRS. FAIRFAX. Aye, dead as the stones.

JANE. Good God. And what of Mr. Rochester.

MRS. FAIRFAX. After his wife had—well, he started to come down and when he reached the great staircase there was a tremendous crash—everything was falling in, you see. Men rushed in and found him trapped under a heavy beam and were able to loose him and drag him out. But—

JANE. Mrs. Fairfax—tell me.

MRS. FAIRFAX. I never thought I'd live to see it. His hand was crushed. It had to be amputated. And—and he's blind—stone blind.

JANE. He's alive!

MRS. FAIRFAX. Yes, if you can call it such. Miserable and crushed as he is. Jane, why did you run away so? He nearly went mad when he discovered you were gone. He tried to find you everywhere.

JANE. Where is he now?

MRS. FAIRFAX. The old manor house, Ferndean, down below. He stays there with John and Leah. Adele has been sent off to school and I live on an annuity in Millcote now, but come here sometimes in the late afternoon. John will walk him here then. I speak to him sometimes, although he has very little to say. Often, I just watch him, poor man— *(She breaks off—overcome.)*

JANE. Will he come today?

MRS. FAIRFAX. Yes, to be sure. *(MUSIC. JANE agitated and expectant moves away. MRS. FAIRFAX checks her watch.)* He is very punctual. He should be coming just now—ah—I believe—it is he.

JANE. Say nothing, please.

(ROCHESTER makes his way through the ruins. He walks with a cane with JOHN beside though not holding him. There is a patch over ROCHESTER's left eye and his right hand is gone.)

JOHN. You are at the door, sir.

ROCHESTER. I know it.

JOHN. Will you take my arm?

ROCHESTER. Let me alone. *(He slowly feels his way to the bench with his cane.)* Pour me a cup of water. I will sit here a moment before we start back. *(JOHN removes the lid from a canteen and drawing out a small cup, pours the water. JANE approaches JOHN, signaling him to be silent. She takes the cup and slowly crosses to ROCHESTER.)* Give me the water, John. John?

JANE. John asked me to bring the water to you, sir.

ROCHESTER. Who is this? Who is this? Answer me!

JANE. Will you drink your water, sir?

ROCHESTER. Great God! What delusion has come over me?

JANE. No delusion: your mind, sir, is too strong for delusion.

ROCHESTER *(reaching about)*. Where are you? Oh, my heart will stop and my brain burst. *(She takes his hand.)* Her very fingers! If so there must be more of her. *(He pulls her to him.)* Is it Jane? This is her shape—her size—

JANE. And this is her voice. She is all here: her heart, too.

ROCHESTER. Jane—Jane Eyre!

JANE. My dear master—I am come back to you.

ROCHESTER *(crosses away—disbelieving)*. I cannot be so blest, after all my misery. It is a dream; such as the dreams I've had many a night when I have clasped my Jane once more to my heart. But, I wake, and she has fled. *(He trips on the bench. JANE helps him to sit.)*

JANE. There, sir—there.

ROCHESTER. It is you, Jane—you are come back?

JANE. I am.

ROCHESTER. So you are not lying dead in some ditch, then!

JANE. No, sir: I am an independent woman, now.

ROCHESTER. Independent!

JANE. My uncle in Madeira is dead and left me five thousand pounds.

ROCHESTER. What? A rich woman?

JANE. Quite rich. If you won't let me live with you I can build a house quite close and you may come and sit in my parlour.

ROCHESTER. You would stay with me?

JANE. Certainly—unless you object. I will be your nurse, your housekeeper, your companion when you are lonely. I'll read to you, walk with you, wait on you. I'll be your eyes and hands, so cease to look so melancholy, my dear master; you shall never be left desolate as long as I live. *(He is silent. Overcome.)* Have I said too much?

ROCHESTER. No—no—Jane; but more than this crippled and blind shell of a man deserves. If I were what I once was—but—

JANE. Sir, have you a pocket comb about you?

ROCHESTER. No. Why?

JANE. Just to comb out this black shaggy mane. I find you rather alarming when I examine you close at hand. *(She smoothes his hair.)*

ROCHESTER. Am I hideous, Jane?

JANE. Very, sir; you always were, you know.

ROCHESTER. The wickedness has not been taken out of you, I see.

JANE. Your hair reminds me of eagle's feathers; whether your nails are grown like bird's claws yet, I haven't noticed.

ROCHESTER. On this arm I have neither hand nor nails. Ghastly, isn't it, Jane.

JANE. It's a pity to see it, and your eyes, and the scar of fire on your forehead, though I am in danger of loving you too well for all this; and making too much of you.

ROCHESTER. Do you love me, then, Jane?

JANE. Yes, sir.

ROCHESTER. Well enough to marry me?

JANE. Yes, sir.

ROCHESTER. A poor blind man, whom you will have to lead about by the hand?

JANE. Yes, sir.

ROCHESTER. A crippled man, twenty years older that you will have to wait on?

JANE. Yes, sir.

ROCHESTER. Truly, Jane?

JANE. Most truly, sir. If ever I did a good deed in my life or thought a good thought—I am rewarded for it now. To be your wife is, for me, to be as happy as I can be on earth.

ROCHESTER. Because you delight in sacrifice.

JANE. Sacrifice! What do I sacrifice? To be privileged to put my arms round what I value—to press my lips to what I love: is that a sacrifice? If so, than certainly I delight in sacrifice.

ROCHESTER. Jane: I did wrong. I defied God and Divine justice pursued its course; I passed through the valley of the shadow of death. Only lately, Jane, I began to pray, very brief prayers, but sincere. I asked God, if it seemed good to him, to take me from this life that I might be reunited with you—for I was sure you were dead. I longed for you and with all my heart's wishes I cried out your name—Jane! Jane! Jane!

JANE. Did you speak those words aloud?

ROCHESTER. I did, Jane. But, what followed is the strange point. As soon as I had called your name, I heard you answer "I am coming. Wait for me." It was your voice and yours alone, as though you were beside me. And now you ARE beside me.

JANE *(moved, quietly)*. Let me take you home. You must feel hungry. We'll be back just in time for dinner. *(She takes his arm and begins to guide his steps.)*

(MUSIC: The schoolgirl's hymn from the beginning of the play which builds to the end as the COMPANY slowly enters, watching ROCHESTER and JANE's exit.)

ROCHESTER. Do you know, Jane, I have the little pearl necklace, that you left behind, fastened under my cravat. I've worn it since the day you left.
JANE. We will go home through the wood: that will be the shadiest way.
ROCHESTER. I'm not sure if I will give it back to you now.

(They walk out of sight. ALL VOICES triumphantly sing the schoolgirl's hymn—but this time it sounds more like the song of the angels. CURTAIN.

After the bows, JANE steps forward to offer an epilogue to the AUDIENCE.)

JANE. Dear friends, I have now been married ten years. I know what it is to live entirely for and with what I love best on this earth. I hold myself extremely blest beyond what language can express. *(She holds ROCHESTER's hand.)* After two years, my husband began to regain vision in his right eye, so that when our first-born son was placed in his arms, he could see that the boy had inherited his own eyes as they once were—large, brilliant and black.

(ADELE joins her.)

Our dear Adele was brought to a fine school near us, where we visited regularly and brought her home often. We have become wonderful companions.

(BESSIE, JOHN and LEAH step forward.)

Bessie came to us and joined John and Leah.

(DIANA and MARY step forward.)

Diana married a captain in the navy and Mary, a clergyman. We see them twice a year.

(BLANCHE walks forward.)

Blanche Ingram married very well, and we never saw her again.

(ST. JOHN walks forward.)

As to St. John Rivers, he left England and went to India. A more resolute pioneer never graced that land. We have written faithfully, though he has never once acknowledged my marriage. He never married himself. I fear the next letter from India will not be in his own hand as illness is taking him very near heaven's door.

(As HELEN and YOUNG JANE come to stand by JANE.)

I hope my blessed friend Helen will be there to hold it open for him. Good night. *(She curtsies.)*

END OF PLAY

NOTES

This dramatization attempts to allow the full scope of Charlotte Brontë's work to be brought to life. Of course, this can't all be literally realized as in a film, so it is imperative that striking images be discovered that will trigger the audience's imagination. If the audience can fill in the gaps, then the venture is successful. Here follow some suggestions for sets and costumes.

THE SETS

THE RUINS OF THORNFIELD. A basic unit needs to be created. Since the play begins and ends in the ruins of Thornfield Hall, an abstract version of chimneys, fireplaces, stairways and door frames can form the basic set. A large empty doorway is a great image for the ruined house. This same door frame, with or without a door, can be used for the exterior of Thornfield at the end of Act One.

GATESHEAD HALL. There are three locations in Gateshead. A hallway, the red room and a sitting room. The hallway can be easily achieved either by very confined lighting or a drapery or traveler can close. This will allow for setting up the bed and bench for the red room, and the furniture for the sitting room. (The red room can be as literal as red walls with a single door and an elaborate bed—or it can merely be a bench in a severe pool of light with the imaginary bed out where the audience sits. The elegant sitting room can either roll on or be assembled by servants.) The whole feeling of Gateshead should be austere and colorless...except for the red room.

LOWOOD SCHOOL. The schoolgirls and teachers can create the four locations here by simply moving benches and tables to different locations. The large classroom is rearranged to become a sickroom. The bed from the red room could be redressed and brought on to be Helen's deathbed. The limbo scene which concludes this section can merely be pools of light with no props or furniture to signify Helen's grave, Brocklehurst's office and a waiting area for the coach. His last scene may need a bench if Jane and Bessie want to sit for their exchange. Again, all austere and colorless.

THE INTERIOR OF THORNFIELD. There are many locations here. The main hall, the library, a sitting room, the music room, Jane's bedroom and Grace Poole's room. One solution is moving platforms that roll in and out to present the different locations. A change of level is good for Jane's room and Grace's room. But, it is also possible to dress several people as servants, including John and Leah and Mrs. Fairfax, and martial them to do furniture changes for the various locations. Draperies which can be opened and closed also allow for furniture to be set up behind and revealed. There are many solutions, and using the same furniture for different rooms is also acceptable if it is true to period. The music room, if it presents a problem, can be eliminated altogether if the first scene is merely offstage—the singing happening outside the parlor and the guests entering when the song is finished. The second music room could be changed to the sitting room and Blanche and Rochester could be playing cards instead of playing the piano. A few effects are nice. The fire in the library can be achieved by using smoke and colored lights. If there are some breakaway draperies this adds a nice touch. It is very nice if Grace Poole's room has a good deal of furniture to hurl around. The wilder and more violent the fight, the more it underlies the animal nature of Bertha.

THE JOURNEY AND MARSH END. Jane's journey can merely be designated once again by pools of light and thunder and lightning effects. When she finally reaches Marsh End a split stage scene is necessary. The kitchen needs a rustic table and benches or chairs and an oven or work area. The parlor opposite requires a settee and desk and chair for St. John. Lighting can distinguish the separation and no real doors are necessary.

MORTON SCHOOL. Once again, the schoolgirls can set up benches and desk for this scene and strike them at the end. There are three different scenes here for which the lighting can suggest passage of time. If you are able to have snow fall for the winter scene it is a nice effect.

RETURN TO MARSH END. It is very nice if on the return the furnishings can be spruced up to suggest Jane has bought some nice things with her money. A few new pieces of furniture, tablecloth, Christmas decorations, etc.

THE MONTAGE. The nightmare which concludes the scene with St. John can be whatever your imagination desires. Placing actors all over various locations in pools of light is effective. If they are recreating moments we remember, this is good also. The one element which can be new is to have Bertha floating through the proceedings wildly. Just as she would have done the night she burned down Thornfield. This is a premonition on Jane's part and something we will very soon learn about in the next scene. We should only hear Rochester's voice, loud and clear above all the others.

FINAL SCENE AT THORNFIELD. It is very important that the lighting for the final scene be warm and inviting. It is a late afternoon and the feeling, even though it is among the ruins, is that Jane has finally come home.

THE COSTUMES

Period authenticity is very important. The number of costume changes is not. If your budget only allows for one or two costumes per character this is fine and, for the most part, except for the Ingram house party, simple is better.

JANE: Dressed in black. She wears a veil which is attached to her hat at the beginning and which she loses once she gets to Thornfield and never wears again. A change of cape or shawl gives her some variety, but since she's barely ever offstage these things generally have to be handed to her. Mrs. Fairfax or Adele are good candidates for that job. In Act Two she needs a simple and lovely wedding gown which she puts on and takes off onstage. Therefore it needs to hook in the front and her undergarments need to be attractive and correct. She can wear the same shoes throughout.

YOUNG JANE: Dressed in black and exact copy of older Jane. She puts a pinafore over this for Lowood School.

ROCHESTER: A rough traveling costume, high boots and a large coat are imperative. He can wear versions of this throughout or have additional changes. He should have a long shirt and dressing gown for the fire in the library scene, a disguise for the gypsy, and evening dress for the party scenes. The evening dress can double for the wedding or a fine authentic suit of the period if affordable. He can wear the same costume for the end that he began the play in except he should wear an eyepatch and his arm should be in a sling.

MRS. FAIRFAX: One black or dark blue housekeeper's dress with a snowy apron and cap.

BLANCHE INGRAM: She should be the most spectacular. If the budget allows she should change for every scene. But if she can at least change her decorative shawls, that gives her a stylish and show-off look. Elaborate jewelry and hairstyle is very important.

MRS. INGRAM, MARY INGRAM, AMY and LOUISA ESHTON, LADY LYNN: The same as Blanche. Stylish party clothes with as many changes or new accessories as possible. The entrance of this group of ladies should quite overwhelm Jane.

LORD LYNN, HENRY and FREDERICK: Fancy evening dress.

ADELE: Charming, fancy day dress and the glittering evening/dance costume (perhaps of rose-colored satin, very short and full; a wreath of rosebuds in her hair, white silk stockings and small slippers) that Rochester presents her. She can alternate in these for the parties or add a pinafore. A new dress for the wedding is nice, but not necessary.

HELEN BURNS and THE SCHOOLGIRLS: Plain uniform of Lowood, perhaps a cheerless high-necked brown dress with a narrow tucker, and workbag at the waist. Helen needs to have a long red wig which she changes to a very short one when her hair is shorn. She should have a shift or nightgown for the death scene.

MISS TEMPLE: Deep purple gown with black trim, if possible. Hair neatly arranged possibly in a snood and her gold watch attached at her waist.

MRS. REED: A handsome gown for her first scenes and nightdress for final scene.

JOHN, GEORGIANA and ELIZA REED: The precious clothes of spoiled pampered children.

BESSIE and ABBOT: Maid's uniforms.

MR. REED'S GHOST: Bed jacket and cap.

MR. and MRS. BROCKLEHURST and AUGUSTA: Handsome fur- and feather-trimmed attire. Perhaps the ladies wear beaver hats with ostrich plumes with elaborate hairstyles. A strong contrast to the drab uniforms of the schoolgirls.

MISS MILLER, MISS SCATCHERD and MADAME PIERROT: Plain, handsome, but spinsterish attire as schoolteachers—Scatcherd is particularly neat and proper.

JOHN, LEAH and other SERVANTS at Thornfield: Matching uniform livery.

GRACE POOLE: Working-class seamstress. Massive and strong-looking in size and bulk.

RICHARD MASON: Traveling coat and broad hat—Caribbean influence. Bloodstained shirt.

BERTHA: Flowing nightdress. Wild, unruly hair.

WOODS: Typical clergyman with surplice.

BRIGGS: Business suit.

HANNAH, WOMEN on ROAD: Farm, peasant attire.

DIANA and MARY RIVERS: Charming simple dresses and attractive hairstyles, shawls.

ST. JOHN RIVERS: Dashing preacher, suit, coat, hat—handsome, romantic.

ROSAMUND OLIVER: Very handsome riding habit, hat, veil, crop and lovely hair falling in tresses.

MUSIC and SOUND

The background music plays an important role setting the mood and atmosphere of *Jane Eyre*. The original score by Albert Evans was very successful, especially his hymn "Walk With Me"* which became thematic to not only the schoolgirl experience, but Jane's journey of faith. The author strongly suggests using Mr. Evans' entire score which can be arranged by contacting: Albert Evans c/o Paper Mill Playhouse, Brookside Drive, Millburn NJ 07041. As an alternative, you may establish as much integrated and meaningful music of your choice as suits your production.

The sound effects are equally important: the cawing of rooks, thunder, Pilot's offstage barking, Rochester's horse, carriages, harpsichord, wind, rain, etc.

*See back of book for this hymn and "The Fairies' Song.")

PROP LIST (as in the Paper Mill production)
ACT ONE

THORNFIELD - 1830ish
Bench (stone/outdoor)
Book ("Bewick's History of British Birds") - YOUNG JANE

GATESHEAD
Hall bench (upholstered)
Pictures (reproductions)

RED ROOM
Bed (unmakes and makes itself)
Bed dressing (pillows, blankets - 2)
Lamp - MRS. REED
Key (to the red room) - ABBOT

HALLWAY
Straw doll - BESSIE (for JANE)

GATESHEAD PARLOR
Fireplace
Fireplace screen
Fireplace tools/dressing
Painting over fireplace
Candelabra (on fireplace)
Throne chair (with seat cushion)
Chaise
Tea table (with tablecloth)
Small table (end of chaise)
Lap blanket (dark-colored, on chaise) - JOHN REED
Lamp (on table)
Rug

Dressing (items showing wealth)
Cups of tea and saucers (2)
Ledger/accounting book - ELIZA
Checkbook - MRS. REED
Pen and ink - MRS. REED
Candy box (with edible chocolates) - GEORGIANA
Game table
Side chairs (2)
Candelabras on fireplace
Sewing box (by tea table)
Torchiere (standing behind game table)
Tile game (set up on game table)
Candy dish (on butler table)
Tray (with cream scones)
Abacus
Book ("Child's Guide") - BROCKLEHURST
Walking stick - BROCKLEHURST

LOWOOD SCHOOL

Book - HELEN
Benches (6)
Stools (2)
Small table (with globe)
Table/desk (with drawers)
Hand bell (hidden in costume) - MISS MILLER
Placard (4" x 15" blank) - on table
Chalk necklace - SCATCHERD
Pointer/switch - SCATCHERD
Trays (2) (with bread and cheese for 16)
Scissors - on table
Doctors bag
Blankets (3) (gray wool)
Sheets/pillows (3 sets)
Workbags (15) (prayer books, sewing kits. Slate and pencils)

Basin with pitcher
Sponge
Chalk
Eraser
Globe
Breakaway slate
Blackboard easels (2) (carried on by actors)

MISS TEMPLE'S ROOM
Bed
Bed dressing (sheets, comforter with cushion, at least 6 pillows)
Side table
Chair
Bunch of wildflowers - YOUNG JANE
Doll
Basin (with pitcher)
Candle/handheld (with flicker candle and globe)
Doctors bag
Measuring string
Small notebook
Helen's headstone
Flowers - JANE
Gold or pearl watch - MISS TEMPLE
Large satchel - JANE
Small satchel - JANE

THORNFIELD HALL
Paintings (6) (large oval and square)
Luggage - JANE
Lanterns (2) (handheld/globed/flicker lights) - SERVANTS
Drape (in one, on rings, pulled open)
Runner on stair
Chandelier (draped in this scene)

Suit of armor
Grandfather clock
Shields on wall

LIBRARY
Fireplace
Fireplace tools
Drapes (catch on fire)
Fire effect (FX)
Chaise (made-up like a bed)
Throw pillows (2) (on chaise)
Chaise end table (2 ft. square, stand L end of chaise)
Sheets and blankets
Throne chair
Butlers tables (2) (low and tall)
Ottoman
Rug
Tea table
Pitcher and basin (on table; water thrown)
Pedestal
Vase with bouquet (water thrown; on pedestal)
Lamp on table
Side chairs (4)
Tea service (tray, pots, cups and saucers)
Cigar box (includes: clipper, ashtray) - ROCHESTER
Matches (strike anywheres, w/ but not in box) - ROCHESTER
Ashtray (w/ but not in cigar box) - ROCHESTER
Ring of keys - GRACE
Tray (with mug of Porter) - GRACE
Riding crop - ROCHESTER
Bowl of soup (w/ spoon) - ROCHESTER
Gift box (lid pulls off) - ADELE
Circlet of flowers - ADELE
Music box (does not really play) - MRS. FAIRFAX

Real candle (on a candlestick - remnant of fire)
Second set of drapes (put up after fire - different fabric)
Bolt of fabric
Feather duster - LEAH

MUSIC ROOM
Harpsichord
Piano stool
Piano shawl
Music (on piano, seen above top)
Standing candelabra
Settee
Chairs (4)
Pedestals
Vases of flowers (on pedestals)
Table (for refreshments)
Glasses
Dishes (with food)
Bench

PARLOR
Sofa
Sleigh chaise (backless/open)
Matching end tables (2)
Side table
Standing candelabra
Ottoman
Bench (DR) - JANE
Side chairs (3)
Card table
Tablecloth (drapes to floor)
Candelabra on table
Vase
Flower arrangement with rose to break

Needlework - JANE
Cane - ROCHESTER
Cards - LADIES
Chess game - MEN
Picture book - LADIES
Tray of *hors d'oeuvres* - JOHN
Serving tray (holding 10 cordial glasses) - LEAH
Lanterns/candles (handheld in globes)
Chairs (extra for Music Scene)
Candelabra (2)
Book - BLANCHE
Fans (6) - LADIES
Fan - ADELE
Calling card - MASON

LIBRARY-GYPSY SCENE

Throne chair
Tea table
Flower pedestal
Small tables (2) (smaller on D throne, larger on U)
Footstool
Candelabra (2) (on tea table and U small table)
Candles (scattered throughout room)
Mug (to drink from) - ROCHESTER
Bandages
Smelling salts
Sponge
Basin
Letter - BESSIE
Purse - JANE
Money (fifty pounds - a paper bill) - ROCHESTER

RED ROOM
Rosary beads - ADULT ELIZA
Tray of food (w/ plate) - BESSIE
Sewing basket (holds letter) - JANE
Letter

OUTSIDE THORNFIELD
Cigar - ROCHESTER
Lantern (handheld globe/flicker) - MRS. FAIRFAX

ACT TWO

JANE'S ROOM
Bed/dressing
Watercolors (on wall over bed)
Armoire
Mirror (handheld)
Small table - LEAH
Hanger (for dress hanging over door)
Necklace box (holds costume pearls) - JANE
Wedding table with wedding cake and decorations
Candles (on table)
Tablecloth (draped to floor)
Small table/altar (on palette)
Vase and bouquet
Luggage (carried out - 3 trunks)
Side table
Flowers
Veil box
Tray (w/ cup and saucer, biscuit on plate)
Leather satchel
Bouquet of flowers - JANE
Small square of blond (woven lace) - JANE

Small box for blond - JANE
Small prayer book - REVEREND WOODS
Valise/satchel - LAWYER
Marriage registry (marriage certificate) - MASON

BERTHA'S ROOM

Fireplace
Fireplace screen
Items on mantel
Brush
Basin and pitcher
Tea kettle
Tray (w/ bowl of soup)
Carpet (thick-padded)
Bed
Chair (ladder-back)
Ropes (ties hands and legs)

LIMBO

Things for people Jane meets
Handkerchief
Bundle of laundry - LADY
Satchel
Lantern

COTTAGE

Tin lanterns (handheld flickers)
Candle - HANNAH

Living Room

Sofa
Table (U of sofa)
End tables

Fireplace
Fireplace dressing (flies with unit)
Desk w/ chair
Books and dressing (piled on desk)
Rug
Footstool
Armchair
Bible - ST. JOHN
Mending basket - DIANA and MARY

Kitchen
Oven (built-in)
Fireplace dressing
Cauldron (w/ soup)
Ladle (to scoop soup from cauldron)
Earthenware crock/bowl (to drink soup from) - JANE
Table
Tablecloth
Bench (3' x 11" x 1' 6")
Chairs
Pie-making things (mixing bowl, rolling pin, flour, pie pans, flat pie dough)
Gooseberries (to stem)
Bowl/colander (2) (for stemming)

SCHOOL

Stove
Coal shovel and bucket
Benches (4)
Desk
Chair (fits under table)
Drawings
Tabletop easel
Sketch pad

Drawing equipment
Portrait
Items for Girls to carry
Prayer book - ST. JOHN
Small books (11) - MORTON GIRLS
Mail (assorted) - ROSAMUND
Letter (in with other mail) - ROSAMUND
Attendance book (same size as ledger for Gateshead)
Pen (to note attendance)
Small book stack (to dress desk)

COTTAGE

Grandfather clock
Add carpet
Lamps (on tables)
Chairs (for kitchen table)
Holiday decoration (on mantel)
Copper kettle
Items of value (on tables)
Pies
Hindustani book (teaches the language) - ST. JOHN

THORNFIELD

Container for water (w/ strap, cap can be used as cup)
Water - JOHN
Cane - JOHN
Cup - JOHN
Comb - ROCHESTER

ABOUT CHARLOTTE BRONTË (1816-1855)

Born the third of six children to the Rev. Patrick Brontë and his wife, Maria, Charlotte would spend most of her childhood and adult life in the bleak parsonage at Haworth, Yorkshire. This was a desolate area, vast moors, practically treeless, the home itself surrounded on all sides by a graveyard. Her mother would bear six children in seven years and then die of cancer. Her tyrannical father had little to do with the young children, he never took meals with them, and gave over the raising of them to his wife's spinster sister, Aunt Branwell. The older sisters, Maria and Elizabeth, died of tuberculosis brought on by unhealthy conditions at Cowan Bridge School. This school became the model for Lowood School and Charlotte's sister, Maria, was in almost every way, Helen Burns. Charlotte, like Jane, was at her sister's bedside when she died. Now Charlotte, age 10, was the oldest and her two sisters, Emily and Anne, and their brother Branwell would create amazing fantasies inspired by a gift of wooden soldiers from their father. Their imaginary worlds of Angria and Gondal would occupy literally thousands of pages. Branwell, the great hope of the family, would turn out to be a dissipated failure addicted to drink and opium and would die a complete disappointment to his father. Meanwhile, his daughters secretly paid for the publication of their poetry from an inheritance left them by their Aunt Branwell. The poetry, under the male pseudonyms, Currer, Ellis and Acton Bell, sold two copies. Undaunted, they immediately sent out novels to publishers and it was Charlotte's novel, *Jane Eyre*, that was instantly accepted and became one of the greatest best sellers in English history. However, no one knew who the author was since she wrote under the pseudonym. Her father did not even know who Currer Bell was, nor the publisher, all correspondence happening through the mail. Her sisters' novels, Emily's *Wuthering Heights* and Anne's *Agnes Grey*, would also be published and receive moderate success, though the critics absolutely loathed *Wuthering Heights*. The novel would, of course, slowly gain popularity with the public and take its place beside *Jane Eyre*. Emily and Anne died shortly after the publication of their works leaving only Charlotte with her father in lonely Haworth. Eventually Charlotte would give in to marrying a clergyman, Arthur Nichols, who she'd turned down repeatedly, only to discover on her honeymoon that she really loved the man. She returned pregnant, but died before the baby was born, at the age of thirty-nine, in 1855. Mr. Nichols and Mr. Brontë, who hated each other, spent their remaining years together in the parsonage at Haworth. Patrick Brontë outlived all his children and died in 1860. Charlotte's other three published novels are *The Professor*, based on her own infatuation with an older married teacher in Brussels, and *Shirley* and *Villette*. None approached the success of *Jane Eyre*.

The five most successful English novels—in order are:
Great Expectations
A Tale of Two Cities
Vanity Fair
Jane Eyre
Wuthering Heights

20,000 pounds in 1840 would be worth 1.5 million dollars today.

Jane's yearly salary of 30 pounds is now worth $2,250.

"Jane Eyre"

The Fairies' Song

Poem by JANE TAYLOR
Music by ALBERT EVANS

Copyright © 1997 Albert Evans

"Jane Eyre"

Walk With Me
Music & Lyrics by Albert Evans

Copyright © 1997 Albert Evans

DIRECTOR'S NOTES

DIRECTOR'S NOTES

DIRECTOR'S NOTES

DIRECTOR'S NOTES

DIRECTOR'S NOTES